Lecture Notes in Computer Science   11379

Commenced Publication in 1973
Founding and Former Series Editors:
Gerhard Goos, Juris Hartmanis, and Jan van Leeuwen

Editorial Board

More information about this series at http://www.springer.com/series/7412

Natasha Lepore · Jorge Brieva
Eduardo Romero · Daniel Racoceanu
Leo Joskowicz (Eds.)

Processing and Analysis of Biomedical Information

First International SIPAIM Workshop, SaMBa 2018
Held in Conjunction with MICCAI 2018
Granada, Spain, September 20, 2018
Revised Selected Papers

 Springer

Editors
Natasha Lepore
Keck School Medicine
of University of Southern California
Los Angeles, CA, USA

Jorge Brieva
Universidad Panamericana
Mexico City, Mexico

Eduardo Romero
National University of Colombia
Bogotá, Colombia

Daniel Racoceanu
Pontificia Universidad Católica del Perú
Lima, Peru

Leo Joskowicz
The Hebrew University of Jerusalem
Jerusalem, Israel

ISSN 0302-9743   ISSN 1611-3349 (electronic)
Lecture Notes in Computer Science
ISBN 978-3-030-13834-9   ISBN 978-3-030-13835-6 (eBook)
https://doi.org/10.1007/978-3-030-13835-6

Library of Congress Control Number: 2019932167

LNCS Sublibrary: SL6 – Image Processing, Computer Vision, Pattern Recognition, and Graphics

This Springer imprint is published by the registered company Springer Nature Switzerland AG
The registered company address is: Gewerbestrasse 11, 6330 Cham, Switzerland

Preface

Medical information and image processing have been experiencing an accelerated growth worldwide in the past decade, and are reaching all parts of the world. In particular, Spanish- and Portuguese-speaking countries in Latin America, which have a long and rich history of academic and clinical research, are addressing a variety of health-care challenges, both general and specific to the region. The scientific communities in these countries have been growing and have attended and organized a growing number of regional and international conferences and meetings.

In this context, the International Symposium on Medical Information Processing and Analysis (SIPAIM) is a yearly event held in various Latin American cities. Its main goal is bringing together biomedical engineering and medical researchers from the region with a strong interest in image and signal analysis.

This community originated in the late 2000s with a series of collaborative workshops around medical information and image processing. These regular workshops eventually evolved into the International Symposium on Medical Information Processing and Analysis (SIPAIM) in 2009, and resulted in the legal establishment of the SIPAIM society (Sociedad Internacional de Procesamiento y Análisis de la Información Médica) in March 2015. SIPAIM is a non-profit foundation promoting research and academic activities in the field of medical information management and medical imaging by bringing together scientists, engineers, physicians, surgeons, educators, and students mainly, although not exclusively, from Latin American countries.

Through these events, SIPAIM has managed to stimulate the emergence of a growing Latin American network related to medical and biomedical information. We are convinced that including the MICCAI community—with its traditional ingenuity and brilliance—in these discussions will help pave the way to a whole set of new scientific challenges, models, and solutions.

This year, as a preview to MICCAI 2020 to be held in Lima, Perú, MICCAI hosted the first ever MICCAI-SIPAIM Workshop. Its purpose was to present success stories of science, research and innovation stemming from Latin American and to encourage the formation of international academic networks in biomedical research with a strong component in medical information processing. The workshop was highly successful, with two plenary talks and a panel of four experts from Latin America. In total, 14 papers were submitted and accepted as poster presentations after being peer reviewed (single blind/two reviews per paper). We intend to sustainably support this network and its spirit in coming years, both until MICCAI 2020 and beyond.

September 2018

Natasha Lepore
Jorge Brieva
Eduardo Romero
Daniel Racoceanu
Leo Joskowicz

Organization

Conference Committee

Conference Chairs

Natasha Lepore	Children's Hospital Los Angeles University of Southern California, USA
Jorge Brieva	Universidad Panamericana, Mexico
Eduardo Romero	Universidad Nacional de Colombia, Colombia
Daniel Racoceanu	Pontifical Catholic University of Peru, Peru
Leo Joskowicz	The Hebrew University of Jerusalem, Israel

Organizing Committee

Natasha Lepore	Children's Hospital Los Angeles University of Southern California, USA
Jorge Brieva	Universidad Panamericana, Mexico
Eduardo Romero	Universidad Nacional de Colombia, Colombia
Daniel Racoceanu	Pontifical Catholic University of Peru, Peru
Juan David García	Universidad Nacional de Colombia, Colombia
Leo Joskowicz	The Hebrew University of Jerusalem, Israel
Alejandro Frangi	University of Leeds, UK

Program Committee

Oscar Acosta	Université de Rennes 1, France
Carlos Alberola-López	Universidad de Valladolid, Spain
Fernando Arambula	Universidad Nacional Autonoma de Mexico, Mexico
Niharika Gajawelli	Children's Hospital Los Angeles, USA
Alfredo Hernández	Institut National de la Santé et de la Recherche Médicale, France
Marius Linguraru	Children's National Health System, USA
Diana Mateus	Technical University of Munich, Germany
Dehaes Mathieu	Université de Montréal, Canada
Mauricio Reyes	University of Bern, Switzerland
Sinchai Tsao	Children's Hospital Los Angeles, USA
Demian Wassermann	Inria, France

Contents

E-Health

Motor Analysis and Biosignals

Medical Imaging

Identification of U-Bundles Based on Sulcus Morphology

M. Guevara[1(✉)], Z. Y. Sun[1], P. Guevara[3], D. Rivière[1], C. Poupon[2], and J.-F. Mangin[1]

[1] UNATI Neurospin, CEA, Université Paris-Saclay, Gif-sur-Yvette, France
mguevara.bme@gmail.com
[2] UNIRS Neurospin, CEA, Université Paris-Saclay, Gif-sur-Yvette, France
[3] Universidad de Concepción, Concepción, Chile

1 Introduction

It is a fact that the brain cortical folding pattern morphology is specific to each human being. Neuroanatomists think that the folding pattern is strongly related to brain connectivity [1]. As each folding variation implies a specific rearrangement of the different white matter bundles, it also impacts the position of functional regions. This particularity raises an issue for precise brain spatial normalization, as nobody knows how to align brains with different folding patterns. For this reason, in the field of brain segmentation, old fashion approaches relying on a single model, often generated from a single subject or a group's average, cannot overcome the folding variability. Therefore, modern strategies are often built from a multi-subject atlas, which has proven to be a very efficient solution to overcome this difficulty [2]. In order to design an analogous solution for brain mapping, it was recently proposed to restrict statistical analysis to groups of subjects with compatible folding pattern [3], which has been experimented to deal with the impact of the central sulcus morphology on fMRI-based activation maps [4]. Differences in the cortical folding have been proved to be associated with differences in the localization of functional areas. Therefore, we need to understand better how to relate to each other brains with different folding patterns. In this abstract, we propose a new step in this direction: we performed a first attempt to observe an effect of a simple morphological polymorphism related to central sulcus on the underlying U-fiber organization.

2 Method

We studied the impact of the left central sulcus on the neighboring short bundles. The central sulcus is one of the most stable and prominent of the human brain, which makes it can be identified without ambiguity, and it presents a precise structure-function landmark called the "hand knob" [4]. We used 71 healthy subjects from the ARCHI database (23.5 ± 5.2 years old of age; 44 males, 27 females; 68 right-handed and 3 left-handed) [5]. First, the isomap of the central sulcus is calculated with the method

© Springer Nature Switzerland AG 2019
N. Lepore et al. (Eds.): SaMBa 2018, LNCS 11379, pp. 3–7, 2019.
https://doi.org/10.1007/978-3-030-13835-6_1

described in [4], obtaining an axis of variability that goes from a "single knob" configuration to a "double knob" configuration (Fig. 1). After affine spatial normalization, the tractograms (i.e. sets of streamlines) of all subjects were further aligned in order to register all central sulci toward the most neutral sulcus i.e. the one with the shape that minimizes the average distance to the rest. Subjects were then gathered in morphologically compatible groups by dividing the isomap axis into 6 intervals of the same length. Subjects of each group did not overlap between them. To each group we applied a slight variation of the method described in [6] in order to identify reproducible short white matter bundles among the subjects (Fig. 2). Briefly, accordingly to the Desikan-Killiany atlas [7], we selected the ROIs around the central sulcus (namely precentral (PrC), postcentral (PoC), caudal middle frontal (CMF), pars opercularis (Op), superior parietal (SP), supramarginal (SM) gyri) and extracted the fibers connecting each pair of them. Then to the extracted sub-tractograms we applied an intra-subject average-link hierarchical agglomerative clustering in order to identify actual fiber bundles (i.e. fibers with similar shape and position along the gyri). The fiber bundles were then matched across the subjects by means of an inter-subject hierarchical clustering, and at the same time bundles that were no present in at least half of the population were discarded. This results in 6 different "atlases", each one specific to its group. Then a matching across atlases is performed to assign a common label to similar bundles. In order to do that a mean centroid representing each bundle is calculated. First, a centroid from the first atlas (the most to the left in the isomap) is taken. A nearby centroid is sought from the second atlas, within a distance threshold. If found, a new centroid is calculated from these two, which is used to seek a nearby centroid from the third atlas and so on. If no centroid is found in a particular atlas, it is just skipped. Unlike the original method were only two preliminary atlases were matched to keep only reproducible bundles [6], in this case we sought to identify the presence of the bundles among the atlases, therefore those with no matches are kept but labeled with a single different label. Also, for each bundle, the correlation of fiber coordinates from 5 equidistant points (beginning, a quarter, middle, three quarters and ending) with the isomap values was computed.

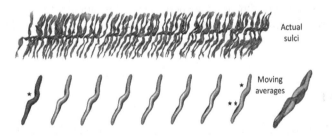

Fig. 1. Moving average of the central sulcus morphology.

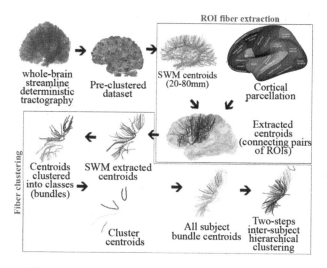

Fig. 2. Schematic of the U-fiber identification method.

3   Results

We computed bundles connecting pairs of 6 regions close to the central sulcus (Fig. 3). From the visual inspection, we identified 6 bundles showing regular changes either in position or shape, along the isomap axis (Fig. 4). Most of these differences correspond to fiber extremities moving up or down as the central sulcus shape shifts. Also, these bundles show a moderate correlation with the sulcus isomap values for at least one section of points, depending on their configuration.

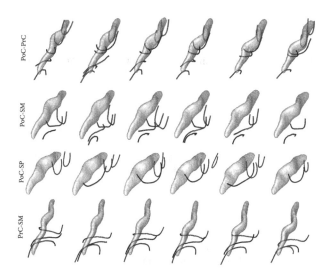

Fig. 3. Bundles obtained with the method.

We also applied the described method to a different database and selected a higher number of atlas. For a same bundle there seem to exist two different configurations among the groups (Fig. 5).

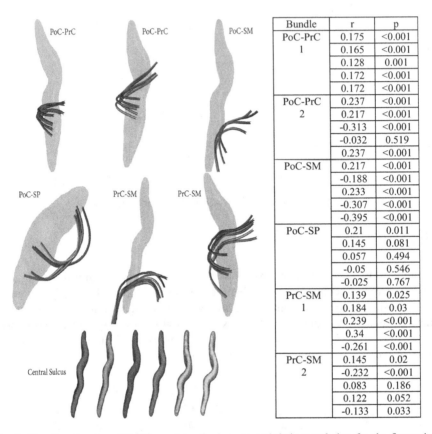

Bundle	r	p
PoC-PrC 1	0.175	<0.001
	0.165	<0.001
	0.128	0.001
	0.172	<0.001
	0.172	<0.001
PoC-PrC 2	0.237	<0.001
	0.217	<0.001
	-0.313	<0.001
	-0.032	0.519
	0.237	<0.001
PoC-SM	0.217	<0.001
	-0.188	<0.001
	0.233	<0.001
	-0.307	<0.001
	-0.395	<0.001
PoC-SP	0.21	0.011
	0.145	0.081
	0.057	0.494
	-0.05	0.546
	-0.025	0.767
PrC-SM 1	0.139	0.025
	0.184	0.03
	0.239	<0.001
	0.34	<0.001
	-0.261	<0.001
PrC-SM 2	0.145	0.02
	-0.232	<0.001
	0.083	0.186
	0.122	0.052
	-0.133	0.033

Fig. 4. Bundles showing differences along the isomap and their correlation for the five points.

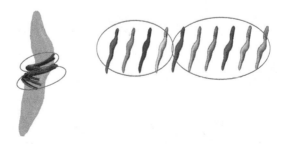

Fig. 5. Results from 10 atlas.

4 Conclusions

We presented preliminary results from the short bundle identification across groups with different central sulcus morphology. These results show that some bundles present different configurations which might drive or come from differences in the sulcus shape. Notice that sometimes, for groups in the extreme of the isomap axis some bundles are not present. Although these bundles might have been discarded during the filtering steps performed, it is interesting as it might be as well because of smaller or even nonexistent connections that impact the shape of the corresponding gyri. However, a better strategy needs to be found in order to ensure that bundles less reproducible within a group could survive until the matching step, as these bundles might present the transition between the two groups. Although these results are preliminary, it shows that there is a link between the brain wiring and the cortical folding pattern. Future work will be focused on testing these differences on a bigger dataset (HCP dataset [8]). This would also allow dealing with more groups which might lead to a smoother transition across the isomap axis.

References

1. Van Essen, D.C.: A tension-based theory of morphogenesis and compact wiring in the central nervous system. Nature **385**, 313–318 (1997)
2. Aljabar, P.: Multi-atlas based segmentation for brain images: atlas selection and its effect on accuracy. Neuroimage **46**(3), 726–728 (2010)
3. Mangin, J.-F.: Spatial normalization of brain images and beyond. Med. Image Anal. **33**, 127–133 (2016)
4. Sun, Z.Y.: Linking morphological and functional variability in hand movementand silent reading. Brain Struct. Funct. **221**, 3361–3371 (2016)
5. Duclap, D.: Towards a super-resolution CONNECT/ARCHI atlas of white matter connectivity. In: Proceedings of ISMRM, vol. 59, p. 3153 (2013)
6. Guevara, M.: Reproducibility of superficial white matter tracts using diffusion-weighted imaging tractography. Neuroimage **147**, 703–725 (2017)
7. Desikan, R.S.: An automated labeling system for subdividing the human cerebral cortex on MRI scans into gyral based regions of interest. NeuroImage **31**(3), 968–980 (2006)
8. Van Essen, D.C.: The human connectome project: a data acquisition perspective. Neuroimage **62**(4), 2222–2231 (2012)

A Method Towards Cerebral Aneurysm Detection in Clinical Settings

Sarada Prasad Dakua[1]([⊠]), Julien Abinahed[1], Abdulla Al-Ansari[1],
Pablo Garcia Bermejo[1], Ayaman Zakaria[1], Abbes Amira[2],
and Faycal Bensaali[2]

[1] Department of Surgery, Hamad Medical Corporation, Doha, Qatar
sdakua@hamad.qa
[2] College of Engineering, Qatar University, Doha, Qatar

Abstract. Cerebral aneurysms are among most prevalent and devastating cerebrovascular diseases of adult population worldwide. The resulting sequelae of untimely/inadequate therapeutic intervention include subarachnoid hemorrhage. Geometric modeling of aneurysm being the first step in the treatment planning, the scientists therefore focus more on segmentation of aneurysm rather than its detection. A successful aneurysm detection among the bunch of vessels would certainly facilitate and ease the segmentation process. In this work, we present a novel method for aneurysm detection; the key contributions are: contrast enhancement of input image using stochastic resonance concept in wavelet domain, adaptive thresholding, and modified Hough Circle Transform. Experimental results show that the proposed method is efficient in detecting the location and type of aneurysm.

Keywords: Cerebral aneurysm · Detection · Hough transform

1 Introduction

Brain aneurysms can happen to anyone at any age and the frequency increases with age. If aneurysms are detected and treated before a rupture occurs, some of the strokes caused by brain aneurysms can be prevented [1]. A brain aneurysm is a weak or thin spot on a blood vessel wall in the brain that balloons out and fills with blood; serious consequences can result if it bursts (ruptures) in the brain spilling blood into the surrounding tissue leading to subarachnoid hemorrhage. Most cerebral aneurysms go unnoticed until they rupture or are detected by brain imaging because of the complexity of brain vasculature anatomy and they always do not occur in a specific region Fig. 1. It is imperative for the patient to be screened by different modalities such as CT with CTA (Computed Tomography with Angiography). CTA images are created by injecting an iodine-based dye into the vein of the arm. As it passes from the vein to the heart and then pumped to the brain, X-rays are passed through the head and images are created. If the clinician does not find the aneurysm and the patient complains again; the

© Springer Nature Switzerland AG 2019
N. Lepore et al. (Eds.): SaMBa 2018, LNCS 11379, pp. 8–15, 2019.
https://doi.org/10.1007/978-3-030-13835-6_2

patient might need to go though CT again exposing him to the repeated radiations exposing the patient to X-ray radiation and iodine which in some patients can lead to an allergic reaction. In order to address this problem, an automatic method for cerebral aneurysm detection would certainly help the clinician find the aneurysm at a go. CTA is performed on multi-detector helical CT scanners that allow multi-planar reformats, sub-millimeter slice thickness, and 3D reconstructions. Several investigators have demonstrated that current multidetector scanners have a spatial resolution that can reliably diagnose aneurysms greater than 4 mm with nearly 100% sensitivity [2]. For aneurysms 3 mm and smaller, early CT technology has been shown to be inadequate, with sensitivity numbers as low as 84% from four-channel multi-row detector CT scanners [3]. Similarly, there are different level of sensitivities, however, the problem of aneurysm is serious since it directly impacts on the nerve system and therefore, it needs to be tackled sensibly. The two main options are endovascular treatment (performed through catheters inserted into arteries under X-ray guidance) and open surgery. The selection of the option depends on many factors: aneurysm location, size, patient condition, patient preference, and local expertise. However, it is important to accurately determine the size, morphology, location, and rupture status of a cerebral aneurysm and/or to identify specific imaging characteristics that may portend a higher risk of rupture so that potential treatment can be guided more accurately. In this paper, we present a novel method by application of Modified Hough Circle Transform & Peak Trekking technique on the image extracted from Computed Tomography with Angiography (CTA). The proposed method is divided into three broad stages: (1) contrast enhancement of input images, (2) adaptive thresholding, (3) template matching, and aneurysm detection by Peak Trekking.

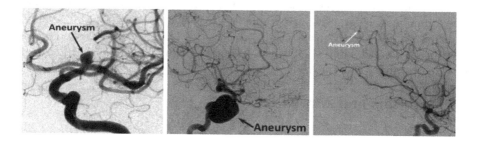

Fig. 1. Samples of brain aneurysm images.

2   Related Work

Over the years, several methods tackle the noisy and cluttered medical images mostly by filtering that leads to degradation in the image quality, therefore in our approach, we utilize the noise in a constructive manner instead. One of the efficient approaches that utilize noise to enhance the contrast of low contrast input image is Stochastic Resonance (SR) [5]. Apart from a few attempts e.g. [4], SR is yet to get the full attention of the image processing community. In this paper, we have applied SR for the image enhancement followed by an adaptive thresholding for image segmentation. SR occurs if the Signal-to-Noise Ratio (SNR) and input/output correlation have a well marked maximum at a certain noise level. Unlike very low or high noise intensities, moderate ones allow the signal to cross the threshold giving maximum SNR at some optimum noise level. In the bistable SR model, upon addition of zero mean Gaussian noise, the pixel is transferred from weak signal state to strong signal state that is modeled by Brownian motion of a particle placed in a double well potential system. In the context of this paper, the double well represents the contrast of an image and the position of particle as the intensity values. The state, at which performance metrics are found optimum, can be considered as the stable state that provides maximum SNR. Some researchers have attempted to use SR in Fourier or spatial domains [4], however we have chosen the wavelet transform domain as explained in the following section.

We use adaptive thresholding that is a function of local property in a neighborhood centered at a pixel location, pixel intensity and pixel location. The literature is quite rich on this [7–9]. However, most of methods are application specific; since we are dealing with medical images, cerebral aneurysm, and the intensity distribution is complex, we have proposed a new method as described in the next section.

Detection of CA from different modalities is a new domain, and has got much to be explored although there have been attempts [11–14]. While McKinney et al. [12] reveal that the combination of DSA with 3D RA is currently the most sensitive technique to detect untreated aneurysms and should be considered in suspicious cases of SAH where the aneurysm is not depicted by 64 multi-slice computed tomography angiography (64 MSCTA), because 64 MSCTA may occasionally miss aneurysms less than 3–4 mm size. Our proposed method makes use of Auto-Thresholding along with Modified Hough Circle Transform & Peak Trekking technique for the accurate detection of CA.

3   Materials and Methods

3.1   Data

The datasets used to test the proposed segmentation algorithm have been obtained from Hamad Medical Corporation in Qatar. On average, each dataset consisted of 400 slices acquired along the long axes of the subjects. The proposed segmentation algorithm is tested on these datasets with average slice thickness of 0.29 mm, pixel spacing of 0.29 mm × 0.29 mm, and matrix size 512 × 512.

3.2   Contrast Enhancement Using Stochastic Resonance

In this methodology, 2-D discrete wavelet transform is applied to the $M \times N$ size image I. Applying SR to the approximation and detail coefficients, the stochastically enhanced (tuned) coefficient-sets in DWT domain are obtained as $W_\psi^s(l, p, q)_{DSR}$ and $W(l_0, p, q)_{DSR}$. The SR in discrete form is defined as:

$$\frac{dx}{dt} = [ax - bx^3] + B \sin \omega t + \sqrt{D}\xi(t) \tag{1}$$

where $\sqrt{D}\xi(t)$ and $B \sin \omega t$ represent noise and input, respectively; these are replaced by DWT sub-band coefficients. The noise term is the cause in producing SR; the maximization of SNR occurs at the double well parameter a. The (1) is solved as in [6] before SR implementation on digital images. The low contrast image may be viewed as a noisy image containing internal noise due to lack of illumination. This noise is inherent in its DWT coefficients and therefore, the DWT coefficients can be viewed as containing signal (image information) as well as noise. The final stochastic simulation is obtained after some pre-defined number of iterations. Given the tuned (enhanced and stabilized) set of wavelet coefficients ($X_\phi(l_0, p, q)$ and $X_\psi^s(l, p, q)$), the enhanced image $I_{enhanced}$ in spatial domain is obtained by inverse discrete wavelet transform (IDWT) given as:

$$I_{enhanced} = \frac{1}{\sqrt{MN}} \sum_p \sum_q X_\phi(l_0, p, q) \phi_{l_0, p, q}(i, j)$$

$$+ \frac{1}{\sqrt{MN}} \sum_{s \in (H, V, D)} \sum_{l=l_0} \sum_p \sum_q X_\psi^s(l, p, q) \psi_{l_0, p, q}^s(i, j) \tag{2}$$

This is the enhanced image after n iterations. The double well parameters a and b are determined from the SNR by differentiating SR with respect to a and equating to zero; in this way, SNR is maximized. This leads to $a = 2\sigma_0^2$ for maximum SNR, where σ_0 is the noise level administered to the input image. The maximum possible value of restoring force ($R = B \sin \omega t$) in terms of gradient of some bistable potential function $U(x)$,

$$R = -\frac{dU}{dx} = -ax + bx^3, \frac{dR}{dx} = -a + 3bx^2 = 0 \tag{3}$$

resulting $x = \sqrt{a/3b}$. R at this value gives maximum force as $\sqrt{\frac{4a^3}{27b}}$ and $B \sin \omega t < \sqrt{\frac{4a^3}{27b}}$. Keeping the left term of this expression to its maximum value and B as unity, $b < \frac{4a^3}{27}$. In this way, the input image is contrast enhanced. An adaptive thresholding method is applied on the contrast enhanced image.

3.3 Adaptive Thresholding

Dynamic statistical parameters are used for estimating the threshold that separates two regions [15]. The dynamic statistical parameters set a low threshold value for high intensity region and a high threshold value for low intensity region. In addition, a change detection technique [16] is used to estimate the position, where the change in intensity occurs. Both methods are combined together forming an adaptive technique to obtain the boundary pixels. In order to discriminate the particles owing to different regions, the individual dynamic statistical parameters viz., mean, standard deviation (σ) and third moment (M) of all the pixels are calculated. The new pixels encountered in the vector update the statistical parameters automatically indicating the change in regions. After each sample pixel, a deciding function DF_f is calculated: $\beta_f = k_1\left(\sigma_f + M_f\right)$. Threshold ($E$) is updated continuously on the basis of the deciding function and is calculated: $E_f = E_{f-1} - k_2\left(\beta_f - \beta_{f-1}\right)E_{f-1}$, where constants k_1, k_2 are determined empirically. In this way, we get as many threshold values as the number of pixels are present. In order to confirm the correct threshold value at the desired location, CUSUM (cumulative sum) [16] is applied. It traps the position of a significant change in amplitude. The boundary pixel is thus given by: $X = \min\left\{f : d_f \geq j\right\}$ and $X = \min\left\{f : D_f \geq r_f + j\right\}$, where D_f is the log likelihood function and $r_f = \min\limits_{1 \leq l \leq f} D_l$. The threshold is compared with the adjacent values to deny any deviation of X from the actual position and the pixel corresponding to both threshold value and X is the *boundary pixel*. In this way, with this process is repeated for all orientations and all the boundary pixels are determined forming a region of pixels enclosed.

3.4   Template Matching

Hough Transform (HT) is a template matching technique that locates shapes in images. HT computation requires a mapping from the image points into an accumulator space or Hough space. Hough transform for circles is chosen as our preferred method of shape extraction since aneurysms are in general of saccular or balloon type. Midpoint Circle Algorithm [10] has been proved to be one of the most efficient algorithms to calculate the pixel positions around a circular path centred at the coordinate origin $(0, 0)$ with a given radius r. A circle function $f_{circle}(x, y)$ is therefore defined in this connection which can be applied in this method is: $f_{circle}\left(x, y\right) = x^2 + y^2 - r^2$.

This generated circle can then be shifted to proper screen position by moving its centre to (x_c, y_c). Modified Hough Circle Transform (MHCT) maps binary image points in I to a 3D parameter space defined as Hough Hierarchy, $\mathcal{H}$. The mapping function for our MHCT algorithm also attributes as Votes casted at co-ordinate point (x, y) is defined as:

$$v\left(x, y\right) = \sum_{r=1} \left[\frac{|\delta\Omega_r\left(x, y\right) \cap I|}{|\delta\Omega_r\left(x, y\right)|}\right] \tag{4}$$

The cardinality operator is used to find the number of pixels. Hough Hierarchy, is generated by the accumulation of the casted votes for all pixel positions within the image: $\mathcal{H} = \left\{(x, y) \in (X \times Y) : \bigcup\limits_{\forall(x,y)} v\left(x, y\right)\right\}$. The co-domain of the function $v(x, y)$ and upper limit of relation $\mathcal{H}$ is given by:

$V = \{0, 1, 2, ..., Heirarchy\ height\}$, where $v(x, y) \in V$ and

$$\max(\mathcal{H}) = \{(x, y) \in (X \times Y), v(x, y) \in H : \max[v(x, y)]\} \qquad (5)$$

Hough Hierarchy associates to every pair (x, y) in $X \times Y$ an element $v(x, y)$ in V. This makes the graph of $\mathcal{H}$ a ternary relation between X, Y and V. Hence, Hough Hierarchy is a 3D parameter space. Hough Hierarchy 3D parameter space resembles a mountain range, therefore, we perform a reverse mapping of the 3D local mountain from the mountain range to a 2D binary region. This process of region detection and region subtraction is iterated till the condition $\max(\mathcal{H}) \geq Peak\ depth$ is violated. Peak Depth decides whether the height of the post processed Hough Hierarchy, 3D parameter space is sufficient for the regions being called as mountain any more

The complete workflow of cerebral aneurysm detection is as follows:

1. The input image if first contrast enhanced.
2. The enhanced image is then segmented using adaptive thresholding method.
3. Hough Circle transform is then applied on the segmented image generating Hough Hierarchy 3D parameter space.
4. Based on the peak, area and compactness, the aneurysm region is detected.

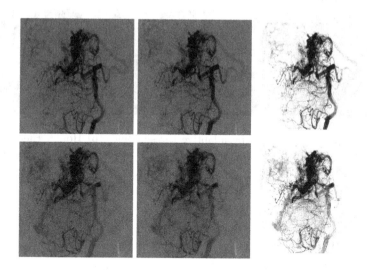

Fig. 2. (a–f) Contrast enhancement of input brain aneurysm images.

4   Results and Discussion

We have tested each stage of the algorithm and included the results although we are not able to accommodate all the results due to page constraints. The results of contrast enhancement are provided in Fig. 2. The results of adaptive thresholding, Hough space, and detection of aneurysms are given in Fig. 3. The average time required by MATLAB R14 to perform segmentation is 2 m for one subject (without optimization). Experimental results have shown satisfactory results for meshes with either simple or complicated model. To evaluate the performance of the approach; performance metrics such as sensitivity, specificity and accuracy are calculated; they are found as 89%, 90%, and 92% respectively. From the Fig. 3, the aneurysm looks like a saccular type. The determination of aneurysm type could assist the clinician in deciding the type of treatment that can be offered to the patient. Although, we have not compared our method with other methods to check its potential level or rank, however, the detection is found quite satisfactory in clinically setting.

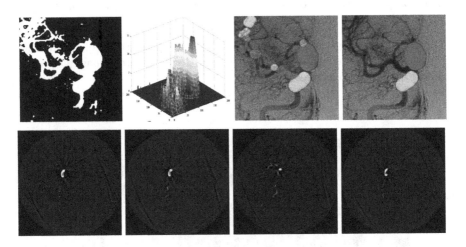

Fig. 3. (a) Simple segmentation by adaptive thresholding. (b) Hough Hierarchy 3D parameter space. (c) Possible aneurysm regions. (d) Final detected aneurysm regions. (e–g) Detected aneurysms.

5   Conclusion

The brain vascular anatomy is huge and complex. Therefore, location and detection aneurysm is paramount before segmentation. Otherwise, the process would be time consuming and there would be higher probability to miss smaller aneurysms that could be present in vascular sub-branches. We have presented a method to detect brain aneurysm in this paper using SR theory, adaptive thresholding, and modified Hough transform. The results are quite satisfactory and promising. In future, we plan to test this method on large database and with other state of art aneurysm detection methods.

Acknowledgement. This work was partly supported by NPRP Grant #NPRP 5-792-2-328 from the Qatar National Research Fund (a member of the Qatar Foundation).

References

1. Alessandro, C., Emanuele, P., Roberto, B., Costa, S.T., Giuseppe, B.: Clinical presentation of cerebral aneurysms. Eur. J. Radiol. **82**, 1618–1622 (2013)
2. Xing, W., Chen, W., Sheng, J., Peng, Y., Lu, J., Wu, X., et al.: Sixty-four-row multislice computed tomographic angiography in the diagnosis and characterization of intracranial aneurysms: comparison with 3D rotational angiography. World Neurosurg. **76**, 105–113 (2011)
3. Teksam, M., McKinney, A., Casey, S., Asis, M., Kieffer, S., Truwit, C.L.: Multisection CT angiography for detection of cerebral aneurysms. AJNR Am J Neuroradiol. **25**, 1485–1492 (2004)
4. Rallabandi, V., Roy, P.: MRI enhancement using stochastic resonance in fourier domain. Magn. Reson. Imaging **28**, 1361–1373 (2010)
5. Chandrasekhar, S.: Stochastic problems in physics. Rev. Modern Phys. **15**, 1–89 (1943)
6. Gard, T.: Introduction to Stochastic Differential Equations. Marcel-Dekker, New York (1998)
7. Issac, A., Partha Sarathi, M., Dutta, M.K.: An adaptive threshold based image processing technique for improved glaucoma detection and classification. Comput. Methods Programs Biomed. **122**(2), 229–244 (2015)
8. Liu, L., Jia, Z., Yang, J., et al.: A medical image enhancement method using adaptive thresholding in NSCT domain combined unsharp masking. Int. J. Imaging Syst. Technol. **25**, 199–205 (2015)
9. Wang, Y.T., Kan, J.M., Li, W.B., Zhan, C.D.: Image segmentation and maturity recognition algorithm based on color features of Lingwu long jujube. Adv. J. Food Sci. Technol. **512**, 1625–1631 (2013)
10. Hearn, D.D., Baker, M.P., Carithers, W.: Computer Graphics with Open GL, 4th edn. Prentice Hall, Upper Saddle River (2010). ISBN 0136053580
11. Hentschke, C.M., Beuing, O., Nickl, R., Tonnies, K.: Automatic cerebral aneurysm detection in multimodal angiographic images. In: Nuclear Science Symposium and Medical Imaging Conference (NSS/MIC), pp. 3116–3120. IEEE (2011)
12. McKinney, A., Palmer, C., Truwit, C., Karagulle, A., Teksam, M.: Detection of aneurysms by 64-section multidetector CT angiography in patients acutely suspected of having an intracranial aneurysm and comparison with digital subtraction and 3D rotational angiography. Am. J. Neuroradiol. **29**(3), 594–602 (2008)
13. Lu, L., et al.: Digital subtraction CT angiography for detection of intracranial aneurysms: comparison with three-dimensional digital subtraction angiography. J. Radiol. **262**, 605–612 (2012)
14. Villablanca, J.P., et al.: Detection and characterization of very small cerebral aneurysms by using 2D and 3D helical CT angiography. Am. J. Neuroradiol. **23**(7), 1187–1198 (2002)
15. Boribhoje, F., Alex, P.: An adaptive real-time ECG compression algorithm with variable threshold. IEEE Trans. Biomed. Eng. **35**(6), 489–494 (1988)
16. Page, E.: Continuous inspection schemes. Biometrika **41**, 100–115 (1954)
17. Singh, T.R., Roy, S., Singh, O.I., Sinam, T., Singh, K.M.: A new local adaptive thresholding technique in binarization. Intl. J. Comput. Sci. **8**, 271–277 (2011)

Common Carotid Artery Lumen Automatic Segmentation from Cine Fast Spin Echo Magnetic Resonance Imaging

Lívia Rodrigues[1]([✉]), Roberto Souza[2], Letícia Rittner[1], Richard Frayne[2], and Roberto Lotufo[1]

[1] Faculty of Electrical and Computer Engineering, University of Campinas,
Campinas, Brazil
lmarodr@dca.fee.unicamp.br
[2] Departments of Radiology and Clinical Neuroscience, University of Calgary,
Calgary, Canada

Abstract. Atherosclerosis is one of the main causes of stroke and is responsible for millions of deaths every year. Magnetic resonance (MR) is a common way of assessing carotid artery atherosclerosis. Cine fast spin echo (FSE) imaging is a new MR method that can now obtain dynamic image data of the carotid artery across the cardiac cycle. This work introduces a post-processing technique that segments the common carotid artery (CCA) wall-blood boundary across the cardiac cycle without human interaction. To the best of our knowledge, the proposed method is the first automatic technique proposed for segmenting cardiac cycle-resolved cine FSE images. The technique overcomes some inherent limitations of dynamic FSE images compared to static images (*e.g.*, lower spatial resolution). It combines *a priori* knowledge about the size and shape of the CCA, with the max-tree data structure, random forest classifier and tie-zone watershed transform from identified internal and external markers to segment the vessel lumen. Segmentation performance was assessed using 3-fold cross validation with 15 cine FSE data sets in the test set per fold, each sequence consisting of 16 temporal bins over the cardiac cycle. The automatic segmentation was compared against manually segmented images. Our technique achieved an average Dice coefficient, sensitivity and false positive rate of 0.926 ± 0.005 (mean $\pm$ standard deviation), 0.909 ± 0.011 and 0.056 ± 0.003, respectively, compared to the majority voting consensus of manual segmentation from three experts.

Keywords: Max-tree · Tie-zone watershed · Carotid artery · Cine FSE imaging

1 Introduction

It is estimated that 4.4 million people die every year because of stroke [14], making it one of the most common causes of death in the developed world.

© Springer Nature Switzerland AG 2019
N. Lepore et al. (Eds.): SaMBa 2018, LNCS 11379, pp. 16–24, 2019.
https://doi.org/10.1007/978-3-030-13835-6_3

Atherosclerosis is a major cause of stroke and is attributed to about 25% of all ischemic events [10]. Currently there are several different types of examinations used to identify carotid atherosclerotic plaques and analyze the artery including ultrasound and x-ray. However, these techniques are generally limited by poor blood-wall image contrast [4,9]. Magnetic resonance (MR) imaging provides improved tissue contrast between vessel wall and lumen [14].

For this project we used cine fast spin echo (FSE) imaging, which differs from usual FSE imaging in that this method collects dynamic information about distension and contraction of carotid artery over the cardiac cycle. Standard MR imaging techniques usually acquire images with good tissue contrast, however, they can be affected by motion artifacts, particularly when needing long acquisition times [9]. Cine FSE imaging, on the other hand, is capable of acquiring a set of N of images (N usually between 10 and 20) over the cardiac cycle in approximately the same acquisition time used by a standard FSE technique to acquire one static image [4,9].

Current carotid artery segmentation methods [2,11,13] use static carotid MR images *i.e.*, there is no temporal information. In addition in most published methods, some degree of human interaction is required. In the present work, we focus on a fully automatic segmentation of the common carotid artery (CCA) lumen, *i.e.*, the interior of the CCA, from cine FSE images. Our segmentation method uses the max-tree [12] area signature analysis combined with tie-zone watershed [3] and random forest classifier [5] to achieve accurate segmentations.

This paper is organized as follows: Sect. 2 describes cine FSE image and proposed solution. Section 3 details the data set and experiments. Sections 4 and 5 present results, discussions and conclusions of this paper.

2 Materials and Methods

2.1 Cine FSE Images

Conventional static MR FSE imaging techniques generate images with acceptable vessel wall-blood image contrast and allows for the depiction of vessel wall morphology and characterization of plaque components. FSE images, with proton density-, T1- and/or T2-weightings are commonly used [10,14]. These images provide only a snap-shot (*i.e.*, they are time averaged) of the vessel wall morphology and composition over the cardiac cycle. They can also suffer from cardiac motion-induced artifacts due to their long data acquisition times [9]. Cine FSE imaging is a new technique that is capable of acquiring images across the cardiac cycle in total acquisition times similar to those required for a standard static FSE technique, albeit often with slightly reduced spatial resolution [4,9]. Because cine FSE images are resolved over the cardiac cycle they potentially can increase its accuracy and reduce image artifacts due to blood flow and wall motion [4].

Cine FSE acquires data over the entire acquisition window asynchronously with respect to the contraction of the heart. The acquired raw MR data is however tagged with its acquisition time within the cardiac cycle (typically using information from a pulse oximeter). The raw data is then rebinned into N temporal bins that evenly cover the average cardiac cycle. N is user selectable and in this study $N = 16$. Because the raw MR data was collected asynchronously, each rebinned data set will, in general, be incomplete. Therefore sophisticated, non-linear reconstruction methods, based on compressed sensing [8], are required to generate images. Compared to static FSE images, cine FSE images are able to generate a similar range of image contrasts (weightings), with potentially lower resolution and signal-to-noise, but fewer flow and motion artifacts. The cine FSE data acquisition process is fully explained in Boesen *et al.* [4] and is a refinement of the method developed in [9].

2.2   Proposed Method

Our solution uses appropriate size and shape information obtained from the max-tree algorithm to find the CCA centroid, internal and external (to the carotid artery lumen) markers, which then are used by the tie-zone watershed transform. The proposed method has five main steps detailed in Fig. 1.

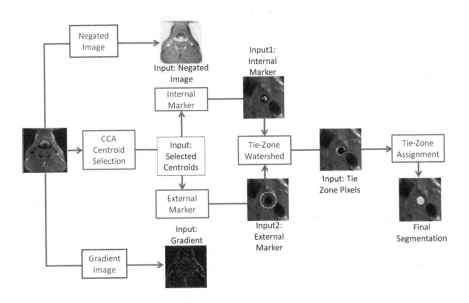

Fig. 1. Flowchart of proposed method.

1. **CCA Centroid Selection:** The first step of the method performs the automatic selection of the left and right CCA centroids. For this task, we use the max-tree for image filtering combined with feature extraction and random forest classification for final selection (Fig. 2).

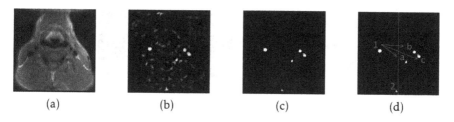

(a)   (b)   (c)   (d)

Fig. 2. Illustration of the centroid selection procedure: (a) Original image, (b) probability image (c) binary image, and (d) Final 6 pairs of centroids: 1-a, 1-b, 1-c, 2-a, 2-b and 2-c.

(a) *Max-Tree Filtering:* Initially, we use a max-tree filter to return only the nodes with area between $14.5\,\mathrm{mm}^2$ and $46.6\,\mathrm{mm}^2$ [7]. This filter is applied over all 16 temporal bins reconstructed by the cine FSE sequence.

(b) *Probability Image and Binary Image:* A probability image is created by summing over all 16 filtered images from the previous step. Next, we applied a threshold of 0.8 to the probability image, therefore maintaining only pixels that appeared in more then 80% of the 16 filtered images, resulting in a binary image containing the candidate nodes (Fig. 2).

(c) *Feature Extraction:* Using the binary image, we perform feature extraction from its connected components (CCs), which are the "white islands" in the binary image. The attributes analyzed consist of the corresponding gray level in the original unfiltered image, area, eccentricity, centroid of CCs and distance between pairs of CCs. In order to create a feature matrix, we divided the final image into a left side and right side and analyzed the identified structures by pairs (Fig. 2(d)). At the end of this step, we have a feature matrix of dimension $n \times 11$, with n being the number of candidate pairs returned in the image. The feature matrix is the input to the classifier.

(d) *Classifier:* We use a random forest (RF) classifier with 45 estimators, operating with entropy criteria to automatically detect the centroids. The classifier outputs probabilities for each candidate pair of centroids. The pair with highest probability is considered the carotid centroids'.

2. **Internal Marker Selection:** The internal marker (IM) selection uses *a priori* knowledge of carotid artery area and one assumption about cine FSE images. These assumptions are: (1) the carotid artery diameter varies from 4.4 mm to 7.7 mm [7] and (2) the histogram of two consecutive temporal images are similar (Fig. 3(f).) In selecting the IM we are interested in the carotid lumen which is dark in the cine FSE image. Therefore, we built the max-tree of the negative image (*i.e.*, the min-tree), then, we analyzed the min-tree area signature starting from the selected centroid to the min-tree root. Finally, we created a filter using *a priori* knowledge about the CCA area ($14.5\,\mathrm{mm}^2$ to $46.6\,\mathrm{mm}^2$ [7]), reducing the number of max-tree nodes that need to be analyzed (Fig. 3(a–e)). From the final candidate nodes, the IM was selected based on our histogram similarity assumption. We selected

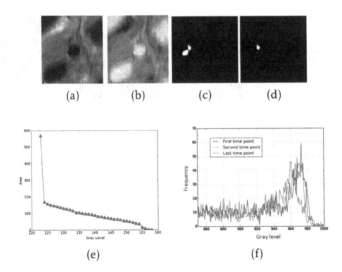

Fig. 3. (a) Original image (b) Negated image (c) Image representing the node before the decrease in max-tree signature, see (e). (d) Image representing the node after the decrease in max-tree signature. (e) Max-tree signature from the negated image for structures smaller then $46.6\,\text{mm}^2$. After the decrease, only the carotid artery lumen and wall are represented. (f) Intensity histograms for region around carotid artery from the same slice at different time points (Kolmogorov-Smirnov test found no significant differences between the three histograms, $p = 0.918$).

as an IM marker the candidate with gray-level value closest to the gray level of the previous time point. For the first temporal bin, we selected the node with gray level closest to the peak value of the histogram, assuming that the vessels are the brightest structures in the negated image.

3. **External Marker Selection:** For external markers (EM), we are interested in the vessel wall, which is the brighter structure immediately surrounding the lumen (Fig. 4). To select the EM, we built the max-tree of the gradient image to find nodes around the carotid artery lumen. We use the gradient image because it accentuates the artery wall-lumen boundary. We choose the node whose centroid has the smallest Euclidean distance to the CCA centroid. Usually, the carotid artery wall is not entirely represented by a single max-tree node (*cf.* Figure 4(b)). The EM will work better if it encloses the carotid lumen; therefore, the final EM was composed of a circle of diameter equal to $1.5\times$ the largest distance between the pixels of the selected max-tree node and the CCA centroid. The selected diameter was not allowed to exceed 7.7 mm, the assumed maximum diameter for the CCA [7], in order to prevent leakage into the tie-zone watershed transform.

4. **Tie-Zone Watershed:** The tie-zone watershed transform receives the automatically selected IM and EM as input and it is applied to the gradient image. The tie-zone watershed returns regions of doubt that have the same cost value for both the lumen and vessel wall labels. These pixels, known as "tie-zone"

(a)   (b)

Fig. 4. Two illustrative cases for finding the external marker (EM): (a) Case where a Node represents the entire vessel wall (green) and the final external marker (blue). (b) Case where there is no node representing the entire vessel wall (green) and the final external marker (blue). (Color figure online)

pixels, need to be correctly assigned in order to improve the accuracy of the method.

5. **Tie-Zone Assignment:** The tie-zone pixels are assigned using a RF classifier with 30 estimators, operating with entropy criteria. The classification was performed on a pixel-by-pixel basis using features extracted from each tie-zone pixel (local binary pattern (LBP) [1], histogram of gradients (HOG) [6], tie-zone labels histogram, gray level of the pixel and mean gray level of 8-neighbors around the pixel). The two histograms (tie-zone histogram and HOG) were computed on a 3×3 pixel window centered about the tie-zone pixel. All features were computed on the original cine FSE image.

3   Experimental Setup

Our data set is composed of 9 healthy subjects, each subject having 5 different MR image acquisitions. Therefore, we have a total of 45 data sets, each with $N = 16$ temporal bins and a resolution of $0.6\,\mathrm{mm} \times 0.6\,\mathrm{mm} \times 2.0\,\mathrm{mm}$. We performed two experiments to validate our proposed method: the first related to the automatic centroid selection and the second related to the CCA lumen segmentation.

Experiment 01 - CCA Centroid Selection: For the CCA centroid selection we used 20 data sets for training and validation of the RF classifier and 25 data sets for testing the classifier. On the training and validation set, we applied data augmentation by applying scale, rotation, and translation transformations to the images, in order to increase the classifier robustness. After data augmentation, our training and validation data set was composed of 105 image data sets. The centroid selection was assessed through the classifier accuracy. The test set and training/validation set were composed by different subjects images, in order to avoid bias towards high performance results.

Experiment 02 - CCA Lumen Segmentation: In the CCA lumen segmentation experiment we used a k-fold, with $k = 3$, cross-validation to assess our method. Each of the folds is composed of 15 images from 3 different subjects. For each image data set we obtained manual segmentation from three different experts

(Experts 1, 2 and 3) for validation purposes of our method. A majority voting consensus was used to assess our results. We used the Dice coefficient, sensitivity and false positive rate (FPR) metrics.

4   Results and Discussion

In the centroid selection experiment, we achieved an accuracy of 100%. In some cases more than one pair of candidate nodes had a probability higher than 50%, but by selecting only the pair with highest probability, this issue was overcome.

For the segmentation experiment, the average and standard-deviation of the cross-validation results are summarized in Table 1. Overall, good visual agreement was observed between our method and the voting consensus of the experts' segmentation (Fig. 5). Our Dice coefficient was 0.926 when assessed against the voting consensus results. Similarly good performance was observed for sensitivity and FPR. [13] reported a dice coefficient of 0.93 when using static FSE images. Despite a marginally lower Dice coefficient, our findings are encouraging because they account for the fact that our data set is more challenging as cine FSE images have lower resolution, and our method is fully automated. Perhaps not surprising given the newness of the cine FSE [4]. We could not find any public segmentation method to directly compare with our method.

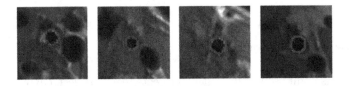

Fig. 5. Representative images. Our segmentation (shown in green) agrees with the voting consensus (in blue). (Color figure online)

Table 1. Dice coefficient, sensitivity and false positive rate (FPR) metrics. Averages (mean ± standard deviation shown) across all three folds are reported comparing automatic segmentation (AS) against the manual segmentation majority voting consensus (VC) and the three experts (Exp m, $m = 1$, 2, or 3).

	Dice	Sensitivity	FPR
AS x VC	0.926 ± 0.005	0.909 ± 0.011	0.056 ± 0.003
AS x Exp 1	0.906 ± 0.011	0.923 ± 0.005	0.057 ± 0.003
AS x Exp 2	0.905 ± 0.009	0.896 ± 0.010	0.084 ± 0.007
AS x Exp 3	0.914 ± 0.004	0.900 ± 0.013	0.071 ± 0.009
Exp 1 x Exp 2	0.918 ± 0.008	0.921 ± 0.005	0.075 ± 0.005
Exp 1 x Exp 3	0.941 ± 0.006	0.941 ± 0.004	0.057 ± 0.009
Exp 2 x Exp 3	0.908 ± 0.005	0.908 ± 0.011	0.057 ± 0.009

5   Conclusions

This work proposes a new methodology for automatic CCA lumen segmentation. There are a number of MR image-based, vessel segmentation methods described in the literature, however, none operate on cine FSE image data sets. In addition, currently available published segmentation methods are semi-automatic; they require some degree of human interaction. Here, we present a fully automatic method, including the CCA centroid selection step. This work is an initial step of a larger project that intends to study carotid artery distensibility (first in the CCA, but then extending to the carotid artery bifurcation, as well as the internal and external artery branches). Based on these findings, we hope to be able to accurately classify carotid artery atherosclerosis patients as healthy (low-risk of stroke) or unhealthy (high-risk of stroke). Cine FSE images are necessary not only for minimizing movement artifacts, but also for allowing the visualization of expansion and contraction of carotid during cardiac cycle, and measurement of carotid artery distensibility.

References

1. Ahonen, T., Hadid, A., Pietikainen, M.: Face description with local binary patterns: application to face recognition. IEEE Trans. Pattern Anal. Mach. Intell. **28**, 2037–41 (2006)
2. Arias-Lorza, A., et al.: Carotid artery wall segmentation in multispectral MRI by coupled optimal surface graph cuts. IEEE Trans. Med. Imag. **35**(3), 901–911 (2016)
3. Audigier, R., Lotufo, R.A., Couprie, M.: The tie-zone watershed: definition, algorithm and applications. In: IEEE International Conference on Image Processing, vol. 2, pp. II-654-7 (2005)
4. Boesen, M.E., Maior Neto, L.A., Pulwicki, A., Yerly, J., Lebel, R.M.: Fast spin echo imaging of carotid artery dynamics. Magn. Reson. Med. **74**(4), 1103–1109 (2015)
5. Breiman, L.: Random forests. Mach. Learn. **45**(1), 5–32 (2001)
6. Dalal, N., Triggs, B.: Histograms of oriented gradients for human detection. In: IEEE CVPR (2005)
7. Limbu, Y., Gurung, G., Malla, R., Rajbhandari, R., Regmi, S.: Assessment of carotid artery dimensions by ultrasound in non-smoker healthy adults of both sexes. Nepal Med. Coll. **8**, 200–203 (2006)
8. Lustig, M., Donoho, D., Pauly, J.M.: Sparse MRI: the application of compressed sensing for rapid MR imaging. Magn. Reson. Med. **58**(6), 1182–1195 (2007)
9. Mendes, J., Parker, D., Hulet, J., Treiman, G., Kim, S.: Cine turbo spin echo imaging. Magn. Reson. Med. **66**(5), 1286–1292 (2011)
10. Saam, T., et al.: The vulnerable, or high-risk, atherosclerotic plaque: noninvasive MR imaging for characterization and assessment. Radiology **244**(1), 64–77 (2007)
11. Sakellarios, A., et al.: Novel methodology for 3d reconstruction of carotid arteries and plaque characterization based upon magnetic resonance imaging carotid angiography data. Magn. Reson. Imaging **30**, 1068–82 (2012)
12. Salembier, P., Oliveras, A., Garrido, L.: Antiextensive connected operators for image and sequence processing. IEEE Tran. Imag. Proc. **7**(4), 555–570 (1998)

13. Ukwatta, E., Yuan, J., Rajchl, M., Qiu, W., Tessier, D., Fenster, A.: 3-D carotid multi-region MRI segmentation by globally optimal evolution of coupled surfaces. IEEE Trans. Med. Imag. **32**, 770–785 (2013)
14. Yuan, C., Mitsumori, L., Beach, K., Maravilla, K.: Carotid atherosclerotic plaque: noninvasive MR characterization and identification of vulnerable lesions. Radiology **221**(2), 285–299 (2001)

Using Deep Learning to Classify Burnt Body Parts Images for Better Burns Diagnosis

Joohi Chauhan[1], Rahul Goswami[2], and Puneet Goyal[1,3(✉)]

[1] Center for Biomedical Engineering, Indian Institute of Technology Ropar,
Rupnagar, India
`puneet@iitrpr.ac.in`
[2] National Institute of Technology Uttarakhand, Srinagar, India
[3] Computer Science and Engineering, Indian Institute of Technology Ropar,
Rupnagar, India

Abstract. Several deaths occur each year because of burns. Despite advancements in burn care, proper burns diagnosis and treatment of burn patients still remains a major challenge. Automated methods to give an early assessment of the total body surface area (TBSA) burnt and/or the burns depth can be extremely helpful for better burns diagnosis. Researchers are considering the use of visual images of burn patients to develop these automated burns diagnosis methods. As the skin architecture varies across different parts of the body, and so the burn impact on different body parts. So, it is likely that the body part specific visual images based automatic burns diagnosis assessment methods would be more effective than generic visual images based methods. Considering this, we explore this problem of classifying the body part of burn images. To the best of our knowledge, ours is the first attempt to classify burnt body part images. In this work, we consider 4 different burnt body parts: face, hand, back, and inner arm, and we present the effectiveness of independent and dependent deep learning models (using ResNet-50) in classifying the different burnt body parts images.

Keywords: Burns · Body part images · Burnt images classification · Burns diagnosis · Deep learning

1 Introduction

Burns are amongst the severe global health issues, and as per WHO Burns Reports 2018, an estimated 180,000 persons lose their life because of burns each year [1]. And many more become crippled forever. Just in India alone, more than 1 million get moderately or severely burnt every year [1, 2]. Around 70% burn injuries occur in the most productive age group $(25 \pm 10$ years), and most patients belong to poor socioeconomic strata. Also, the post burn life of burns survivor is never the same - socially, economically, mentally and physically. Timely done burns diagnosis and adequate first aid treatment can check the burns severities and significantly reduce the number of burn death cases. However, there are several challenges such as limited number of expert dermatologists, limited number of burn centres, lack of awareness

N. Lepore et al. (Eds.): SaMBa 2018, LNCS 11379, pp. 25–32, 2019.
https://doi.org/10.1007/978-3-030-13835-6_4

about the first aid and prevention strategies, use of manual methods in diagnosis, and heavy treatment costs. Despite advancements in burn care, proper burns diagnosis and treatment of burn patients remains a major challenge. Automated methods to give an early assessment of the total body surface area (TBSA) burnt and/or the burns depth can be extremely helpful for better burns diagnosis [2–5]. Laser Doppler imaging (LDI) has been found as most reliable technique for burn depth assessment but high costs, delays and limited portability limits its real world usage [4, 6, 7]. Considering high penetrations of Smartphones having good resolution cameras and advances in data sciences, visual images based automated burns diagnosis methods can be very useful.

A group of researchers from University of Seville, Spain had been actively contributing in this domain of burn depth assessment methods using color images from around last two decades [3, 8–10]. Lately, they presented a psychophysical experiment and multidimensional scaling analysis to determine the physical characteristics that physicians employ to diagnose a burn depth [3]. In this work, they used a k-nearest neighbor classifier on a dataset of 74 images, and the accuracy of 66.2% was achieved in classifying the burn images considered into three burn depths with their approach. Earlier, Wantanajittikul et al. described a support vector machine (SVM) based approach for burn degree assessment [11] but they also considered very less images. Recently, Badea et al. [5] proposed an ensemble method build upon fusing decision from standard classifiers (SVM and Random Forest) and the CNN architecture ResNet [12] for burn severity assessment. For feature extraction, they used primarily the Histogram of Topographical features (HoT). Their proposed system was able to identify light/serious burns with an average precision of 65%.

As the skin architecture varies across different parts of the body [13, 14], and so the burns impact on different body parts skin would be different. Therefore, it is likely that the body part specific visual images based automatic burns diagnosis assessment methods would be more effective than generic visual images based methods. Considering this, we explore this problem of classifying the body part of burn images. To the best of our knowledge, ours is the first attempt to classify burnt body part images. In this work, we consider four different burnt body parts: face, hand, back, and inner arm, and we aim to identify the body-part of the given input burnt image. We then discuss the performance of ResNet50 deep learning architecture based independent and dependent deep learning models in classifying the different burnt body parts images.

2 Data Collection

Using Google Search engine, we gathered burned images of different body parts [15–39]. Out of these total 109 burnt images that we collected, there are 30 face images, 35 hand images, 23 back images and rest are inner forearm images. The average resolution of these images is in the range of $(350 - 450) \times (300 - 400)$ pixels. Figures 1, 2 and 3 show some sample burnt images of back, hand and inner forearm.

We also used in one of our models a dataset of 4981 non-burnt skin images of these four different parts: back, face, hand and inner forearm. We used some available datasets for these images [40–43].

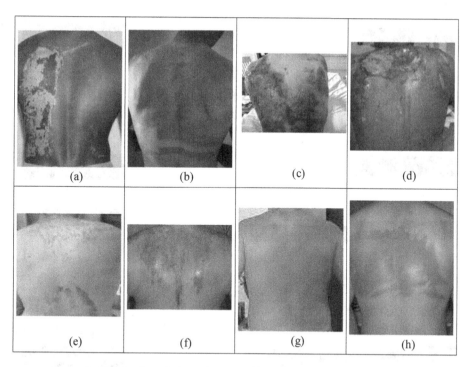

Fig. 1. Sample burnt images of human back body parts

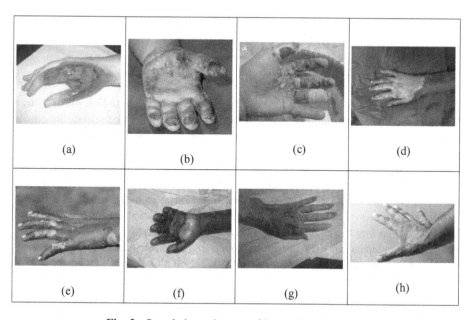

Fig. 2. Sample burnt images of human hand [16–39]

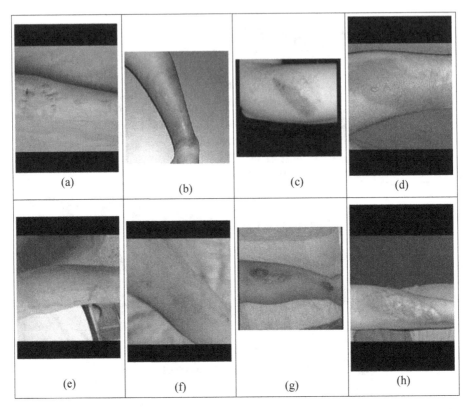

Fig. 3. Sample burnt images of inner forearm [16–39]

3   Methodology

We use the ResNet50 architecture deep learning models (as shown in Fig. 4) for feature extraction [12]. We freeze all the layers of the ResNet-50 model and replace its output layer by a dense layer with 4 nodes, representing 4 classes. The average pooling method is used for feature extraction. We use Softmax activation function, ADAM optimizer and categorical cross-entropy loss function in our model. We used two variants of this model: M1 - dependent and M2 - independent (considering limited number of burn images), for the classification of the body-part of the input burnt image.

For dependent model M1, we used leave-one-out cross validation (LOOCV) for classification. Noting the challenge of limited number of burnt images availability, we explored the independent deep learning model and its effectiveness for this classification problem. In the independent model M2, we used a total of 4981 non-burnt skin images of four different parts (face images: 2000 [40], hand images: 2000 [41], back: 81 [42], and inner forearm: 800 images [43]) for the training, a total of 1798 non-burnt skin images for the validation [40–43], and the same 109 burnt body part images for the testing. To account for class imbalance in training, we normalized the class weights to be inversely proportional to number of images in that class.

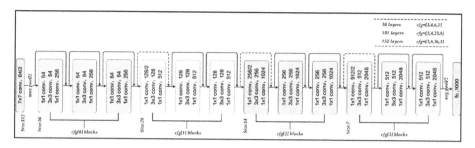

Fig. 4. Block diagram of the ResNet50 architecture used [44]

4   Experimental Results

For the 109 burnt body parts images, we obtained overall classification accuracy of 90.83% and 93.58% using dependent (M1) and independent (M2) deep learning ResNet-50 model, respectively. The M1 used LOOCV and thus training was performed 109 times. It accurately classified 22 back body part burn images, 27 face images, 31 hand images and 19 inner forearm burnt images.

Table 1. Classification accuracy results.

Classes	No. of images	M1: classification accuracy (%)	M2: classification accuracy (%)
Back	23	**95.65**	91.3
Face	30	90	**96.67**
Hand	35	88.57	**97.14**
Inner forearm	21	**90.48**	85.71
Total	**109**	**90.83**	**93.58**

The model M2 that was trained using no burn images classified in comparison 2 back and 3 forearm burnt image inaccurately, but M2 performed much better in classifying other body-parts burnt images as 29 face and 34 hand burnt images were classified accurately (Tables 2 and 3). Table 1 presents the classification accuracy results and effectiveness of these two models. When we consider the top 2 estimated classes for each of the test image, both the models were found to be more than 99% accurate.

Table 2. Confusion matrix for model M1

Actual	Predicted			
	Back	Face	Hand	Inner forearm
Back	22	0	1	0
Face	2	27	1	0
Hand	4	0	31	0
Inner forearm	1	0	1	19

Table 3. Confusion matrix for model M2

Actual	Predicted			
	Back	Face	Hand	Inner forearm
Back	21	0	2	0
Face	1	29	0	0
Hand	1	0	34	0
Inner forearm	0	0	3	18

5   Conclusions and Future Work

We discussed a new problem of classifying burnt body part images that can help in the development of better burns diagnosis methods and we present the effectiveness of some deep learning models in addressing this problem, considering the constraint of limited number of burnt images availability. It is encouraging and interesting to note that a ResNet50 architecture based model, trained using non burnt images, was able to classify with more than 93% accuracy the burnt images of 4 different body parts: face, back, hand, and inner forearm. Further, there is a scope of exploring the robustness and effectiveness of the proposed method using much larger number of burnt images and considering more classes by including other body parts e.g. feet, stomach or chest.

References

1. Burns (2018). http://www.who.int/mediacentre/factsheets/fs365/en/. Accessed 28 June 2018
2. A WHO plan for burn prevention and care Geneva: World Health Organization (2008). http://apps.who.int/iris/bitstream/10665/97852/1/9789241596299_eng.pdf. 28 June 2018
3. Acha, B., Serrano, C., Fondon, I., Gomez-Cia, T.: Burn depth analysis using multidimensional scaling applied to psychophysical experiment data. IEEE Trans. Med. Imaging **32**(6), 1111–1120 (2013)
4. Pape, S.A., Skouras, C.A., Bryne, P.O.: An audit of the use of laser doppler imaging (LDI) in the assessment of burns of intermediate depth. Burns **27**, 233–239 (2001)
5. Badea, S. M, Vertan, C., Florea, C., Florea, L., Bădoiu, S.: Severe burns assessment by joint color-thermal imagery and ensemble methods. In: IEEE HealthCom (2016)
6. Monstrey, S., Hoeksema, H., Verbelen, J., Pirayesh, A., Blondeel, P.: Assessment of burn depth and burn wound healing potential. Burns **34**(6), 761–769 (2008)
7. Wearn, C., et al.: Prospective comparative evaluation study of laser doppler imaging and thermal imaging in the assessment of burn depth. Burns **44**(1), 124–133 (2018)
8. Roa, L., Gómez-Cía, T., Acha, B., Serrano, C.: Digital imaging in remote diagnosis of burns. Burns **25**(7), 617–624 (1999)
9. Acha, B., Serrano, C., Roa, L.: Segmentation and classification of burn color images. In: Proceedings of the 23rd Annual International Conference of the IEEE Engineering in Medicine and Biology Society, vol. 3 (2001)
10. Carmen, S., Rafael, B.-T., Gomez-Cia, T., Acha, B.: Features identification for automatic burn classification. Burns **41**, 1883–1890 (2015)

11. Wantanajittikul, K., Theera-Umpon, N., Auephanwiriyakul, S., Koanantakool, T.: Automatic segmentation and degree identification in burn color images. In: Biomedical Engineering International Conference (BMEiCON), pp. 169–173 (2012)
12. He, K., Zhang, X., Ren, S., Sun, J.: Deep residual learning for image recognition. In Proceedings of the IEEE Conference on Computer Vision and Pattern Recognition (2016)
13. Adabi, S., et al.: Universal in vivo textural model for human skin based on optical coherence tomograms. Sci. Rep. **7** (2017)
14. Langer, K.: On the anatomy and physiology of the skin. Br. J. Plast. Surg. **31**(1), 3–8 (1978)
15. www.google.com. Accessed 03 Aug 2018
16. www.pinsdaddy.com/. Accessed 03 Aug 2018
17. www.Ytimg.com. Accessed 03 Aug 2018
18. www.istockphoto.com. Accessed 04 Aug 2018
19. www.dailystar.co.uk/real-life/459698/Rare-skin-conditions-third-degree-burns-inspirational-man. Accessed 04 Aug 2018
20. www.deviantart.com/arrowkitillashwood/art/Third-Degree-Burns-271699844. Accessed 04 Aug 2018
21. http://asktheburnsurgeon.blogspot.com/p/burn-pictures-and-videos.html. Accessed 04 Aug 2018
22. http://practicalplasticsurgery.org/2011/05/case-3-hand-injury-severe-burn-scar-contracture/. Accessed 04 Aug 2018
23. https://burnssurgery.blogspot.com/2012/01/?view=classic. Accessed 04 Aug 2018
24. www.dalafm.co.ke/a-woman-burns-her-grandson-in-siaya/news/county-news/. Accessed 30 July 2018
25. https://lekton.info/plus/t/third-degree-skin-burns/. Accessed 31 July 2018
26. http://styleupnow.com/beauty-tips-4-simple-ways-to-treat-burns-at-home/. Accessed 31 July 2018
27. https://salamanders.neocities.org/burnface.htm. Accessed 31 July 2018
28. http://olivero.info/bari/f/first-degree-burns-on-face/. Accessed 31 July 2018
29. www.thinglink.com/scene/716464757611167744. Accessed 31 July 2018
30. www.cyclingweekly.com/news/chris-froomes-mesh-skinsuit-sunburn-18852. Accessed 31 July 2018
31. www.dreamstime.com/stock-photo-burn-sun-body-human-back-burnt-sunburn-scald-back-s-beams-image97972700. Accessed 31 July 2018
32. commons.wikimedia.org/wiki/File:1Veertje_hand_burn.jpg. Accessed 30 July 2018
33. http://makeupbygill.blogspot.com/2011/10/special-effects-burns-assessment.html. Accessed 30 July 2018
34. www.derma-gel.net/case-studies/second-degree-burn-face/. Accessed 30 July 2018
35. csn.cancer.org/node/262311. Accessed 28 July 2018
36. www.thepinsta.com. Accessed 28 July 2018
37. http://1s-pozycjonowanie-narzedzia.info/2rd-degree-burn-pictures.html. Accessed 20 June 2018
38. www.enews.tech/chemical-burns-on-hands.html. Accessed 02 Aug 2018
39. http://obryadii00.blogspot.com/2011/03/pictures-of-2nd-degree-burns.html. Accessed 02 Aug 2018
40. Gourier, N., Hall, D., Crowley, L.J.: Estimating face orientation from robust detection of salient facial features. In Proceedings of Pointing 2004, ICPR, International Workshop on Visual Observation of Deictic Gestures, Cambridge, UK (2004)

41. Mahmoud, A.: 11 K hands: gender recognition and biometric identification using a large dataset of hand images. arXiv:1711.04322 (2017)
42. Nurhudatiana, A., et al.: The individuality of relatively permanent pigmented or vascular skin marks (RPPVSM) in independently and uniformly distributed patterns. IEEE Trans. Inf. Forensics Secur. **8**(6), 998–1012 (2013)
43. Zhang, H., Tang, C., Kong A., Craft, N.: Matching vein patterns from color Images for forensic investigation. In: Proceedings of IEEE International Conference on Biometrics: Theory, Applications and Systems, pp. 77–84 (2012)
44. https://www.codeproject.com/Articles/1248963/Deep-Learning-using-Python-plus-Keras-Chapter-Re. Accessed 31 July 2018

Mixed-Model Noise Removal in 3D MRI via Rotation-and-Scale Invariant Non-Local Means

Xiangyuan Liu[1], Quansheng Liu[2], Zhongke Wu[1], Xingce Wang[1(✉)],
Jose Pozo Sole[3], and Alejandro Frangi[3]

[1] Beijing Normal University, Beijing, China
wangxingce@bnu.edu.cn
[2] Univ. de Bretagne-Sud (South Brittany), Brittany, France
[3] University of Sheffield, Sheffield, UK

Abstract. Mixed noise is a major issue influencing quantitative analysis in different forms of magnetic resonance image (MRI), such as T1 and diffusion image like DWI and DTI. Using different filters sequentially to remove mixed noise will severely deteriorate such medical images. We present a novel algorithm called rotation-and-scale invariant nonlocal means filter (RSNLM) to simultaneously remove mixed noise from different kinds of three-dimensional (3D) MRI images. First, we design a new similarity weights, including rank-ordered absolute difference (ROAD), coming from a trilateral filter (TriF) that is obtained to detect the mixed and high-level noise. Then, we present a shape view to consider the MRI data as a 3D operator, with which the similarity between the patches is calculated with the rigid transformation. The translation, rotation and scale have no influence on the similarity. Finally, the adaptive parameter estimation method of ROAD is illustrated, and the effective proof that validates the proposed algorithm is presented. Experiments using synthetic data with impulse noise, Rician noise, and the real MRI data confirm that the proposed method yields superior performance compared with current state-of-the-art methods.

1 Introduction

In modern magnetic resonance imaging (MRI) reconstruction systems, MRI noise is more complex with a mixed model than the traditional Rician distribution with constant noise power [1,6], involving mixed types of noise. During the transmission, impulse noise will also be generated in MRIs via noisy sensors, communication channels, transmission apparatus, and other factors. Simultaneously removing all these types of noise while keeping the meaningful edges is a crucial problem for medical image processing.

Previous works focus on removing the traditional MRI noise model by the Rician noise with the non-local means (NLM) [2] method, which has exhibited particularly good performance in edge-preserving denoising. Coupé [4] introduced NLM in MRI denoising, and then Wiest used it in a diffusion MRI dataset

© Springer Nature Switzerland AG 2019
N. Lepore et al. (Eds.): SaMBa 2018, LNCS 11379, pp. 33–41, 2019.
https://doi.org/10.1007/978-3-030-13835-6_5

[13]. The key features of NLM are beyond the local-neighborhood, nonlocal, spatial distant information and self-similarity weight involved in the denoising. Recently, Manjón [10] proposed method of prefiltered rotationally invariant NLM3D (Pri-NLM) by combining different filter together. Chen [3] calculated the neighborhood both on the spatial and wave-vector space to obtain a good result. Few papers, however, discuss mixed noise removal and different kinds of weight design.

There are two main models for the removal of the mixture of Rician noise and impulse noise from MRI: removing different kinds of noises in multiple steps or simultaneously. For removal of different types of noise in multiple steps, one common method is to combine a Rician filter with an impulse filter. We integrate the BM4D [9] and median filters, called a BM4DM filter, but the intensity of pixels is often changed by the first filter in that they usually invalidate efforts to remove impulse noise in subsequent steps and vice versa. For simultaneous removal of different types of noise, Garnett [12] introduced the rank-ordered absolute difference (ROAD) statistic for the detection of pixels contaminated by impulse noise and integrated it into the bilateral filter to construct the trilateral filter (TriF [8]). The patch-based weighted means filter [5] improves the TriF by extending the weights in the NLM.

In this paper, we accept the second idea and propose a rotation-and-scale-invariant nonlocal means (RSNLM) filter to remove the mixed noise simultaneously from the 3D MRI data. Our main contributions are threefold: (1) We combine the ideas of NLM and TriF to remove the mixed noise simultaneously for the high self-similarity of 3D MRI data. (2) We consider the 3D patch as a 3D volume shape model of 3D MRI data with extension of the rigid transformation (translation, rotation, and scaling) in graphics to calculate the similarity between 3D patches. (3) We propose an automatic parameter selection of the ROAD statistic, making the algorithm adaptive and efficient to detect and remove high-level impulse noises.

2   Methods

Problem Formulation. Various noises will coexist in MR images, especially Rician noise and impulse noise. Owing to the distribution of impulsive noise, the point destroyed by impulse noise is always clearly different from its surrounding pixels. The noise level of impulse noise is defined by p, the probability that a pixel will be corrupted by impulse noise. It is known that the magnitude of the MRI image is computed from the real image and imaginary image contain Gaussian distributed noise, and the noise contained in the magnitude of the MRI follows a Rician distribution [11]. The main idea behind NLM is to estimate each pixel by a weighted mean of the observed values $v(j)$ for j in search window, $N_i(D)$, with weights depending on the similarity between local patches centered at i and j. More precisely, the NLM filter is defined as

$$\hat{v}\,(i) = \frac{\sum_{j \in N_i(D)} w(i,j)v(j)}{\sum_{j \in N_i(D)} w(i,j)}, \quad \text{with} \quad w(i,j) = e^{-\|v(N_i) - v(N_j)\|_2^2/(2\sigma_h^2)}, \quad (1)$$

$v(N_i)$ and $V()N - j$ are the vectors composed of pixels in N_i and N_j, d^3 patches centered at i and j respectively, arranged in a fixed order. $\|v(N_i) - v(N_j)\|_2$ represents the Euclidean distance between N_i and N_j, which measures the similarity between these two patches. The classic NLM is designed to remove Gaussian noise and needs to be modified for the noncentral Rician noise distribution. Based on [4], we define the unbiased denoised signal as being replaced by

$$\hat{v}(i) = \sqrt{\max\left(\left(\frac{\sum_{j \in N_i(D)} w(i,j)v^2(j)}{\sum_{j \in N_i(D)} w(i,j)}\right) - 2\sigma^2, 0\right)} \tag{2}$$

σ is the noise level. We focus on finding an good strategy to calculate the weight $w(i,j)$ with the similarity of patches in shape view. An overview of proposed method is summarized in Algorithm 1.

Algorithm 1. The RSNLM Algorithm

Require:
 1: Noisy MRI data: I;
 2: The set of hyper-parameter: $\Theta = \{D, d, \sigma_I, \sigma_M, \sigma_S, \sigma_{SM}\}$;
Ensure:
 3: Estimate parameter m in ROAD statistic;
 4: A D^3 search window;
 5: A d^3 similar patch;
 6: **repeat**
 7:     Moving the search window $N_i(D)$ centered at $i \in I$;
 8:     Get the estimative patch $N_i(d)$ centered at i;
 9:     **repeat**
10:         Moving the similar patch $N_j(d)$ centered at $j \in N_i(D)$;
11:         Find $N_i(d)$'s most similar patch by the rigid transformation of $N_j(d)$.
12:         Calculate $w(i,j)$ by Eq. 3;
13:     **until** Traverse all the points in $N_i(D)$.
14:     Obtain the estimation intensity result of pixel $i, O(i) = \hat{v}(i)$
15: **until** Traverse all the points in I.
16: **return** The restored MRI data O.

Weights Estimation in RSNLM. The patch similarity of RSNLM defined in Eq. 3.

$$w(i,j) = w_s(i,j)w_I(i,j)w_{MR}(i,j) \tag{3}$$

Inspired by TriF, we utilize ROAD [12] to detect pixels contaminated by impulse noise. We consider three factors to express the similarity between patches i and patches j with weight $w(i,j)$. With the manifold theory, the local similarity is more reliable than the faraway one. $w_s(i,j) = e^{-\|i-j\|_2^2/(2\sigma_S^2)}$ reflects the influence on spatial distance $\|i - j\|$ between pixel i and pixel j.

$w_I(i,j) = e^{-ROAD(j)^2/(2\sigma_I^2)}$ is an impulse factor, which is close to zero if j is an impulse noisy point or is seriously different from its surrounding pixels. The value of $ROAD$ at pixel j is defined as $ROAD(j) = \sum_{k=1}^{m} r_k(j)$ where $r_k(j)$ is the kth term in the set $\{|v(i) - v(j)| : i \in N_j(R) \setminus \{j\}\}$ arranged in an increasing order with possibly equal terms. If j is a impulse noise or if an impulse noise exists in patch j, $ROAD(j)$ will be very high. w_{MR} is calculated with Eq. 4, which describes the similarity of pixel values in two patches. With all three of these factors, we can detect the impulse noise and high-level Rician noise, and can simultaneously remove them:

$$w_{MR}(i,j) = e^{-(\|v(N_i)-v(N_j)\|_{SR})^2/(2\sigma_{MR}^2)} \tag{4}$$

where

$$\|v(N_i) - v(N_j)\|_{SR} = \inf_{\substack{r \in [0,2\pi] \\ t \in [1,2]}} \|v(N_i) - v(S_t R_r N_j)\|$$

$$= \sqrt{\frac{\sum_{k \in N_0} w_s(j,k) J_I(i+k, j+S_t R_r k) |v(i+k) - v(j+S_t R_r k)|^2}{\sum_{k \in N_0} w_s(j,k) J_I(i+k, j+S_t R_r k)}}.$$

$S_t R_r$ is the rotation of angle r and shrinking t timesregarding the origin 0. Here, $S_t R_r N_j$ denotes the rotation and scaling of N_j regarding its center j: $S_t R_r N_j = \{j + S_t R_r k : k \in N_j^0\}$, where N_j^0 is the most primitive patch centered at j without rigid transformation of N_j. As defined above, $w_s(j,k)$ is used to describe the space distance between j and k, which means that we are more focused on the similarity between the closer pixels. The term $J_I(i+k, j+S_t R_r k)$, as the joint impulse coefficient of $i+k$ and $j+S_t R_r k$, is defined as $J_I(i+k, j+ S_t R_r k) = w_I(i+k)w_I(j+S_t R_r k)$, which is used to remove the influence of impulse noise points in the similarity measure.

Ridge Transformation of the Compared Patch. From shape view, the ridge transformation(translation, scaling, and rotation) of the patch should have no influence on the distance $\|v(N_i) - v(N_j)\|_{SR}$ in Eq. 4.

Translation Invariance. The patch j slides all parts of the window, which eliminates the influence on location of j. **Scale invariance.** In the proposed method, we obtain a small proportion of the original images by taking a morphological transformation, t, which is the reduced ratio. The patch size d of j is $(2^3)^{t-1}$ larger than the patch i. With interlacing down-sampling $t-1$ times, we can eliminate the influence on multi-scale and obtain a more comparative patch. **Rotation invariance.** To complete the rotation in 3D space, we decomposed the process into three 2D

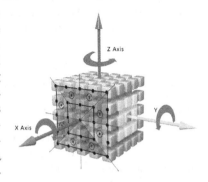

Fig. 1. Rotation diagram

rotations around the three axes (x, y, z), respectively, as shown in Fig. 1. A square can be divided into eight parts (①~⑧), with which the position of the patch can be decided by finding one part's position after the rotation. To minimize $\|v(N_i) - v(N_j)\|_{SR}$ on $r \in [0, 2\pi]$, the discrete solution is to find the minimization over the set of a finite number of angles, for $r \in \{2\pi k/n, k = 0, 1, \cdots, n-1\}$ with $n > 1$ a suitable integer. n is set as a function of the size of cubes $N_i(d)$; in our experiments we choose $n = 4(d-1)$. We set $n = 16$ for $d \geq 5$ for the time complexity.

Adaptive ROAD Parameter. The parameter m in ROAD is an important factor by which to detect the impulse level that should not be constant, as in [12]. We set m as a function of the impulse noisy level p. X, the number of non-impulse noisy points in $N_i(R)$, follows binomial distribution with parameters $R \times R \times R$ and $1-p$. The probability that $X = k$ is $P(X = k) = C_{R \times R \times R}^k (1-p)^k p^{R \times R \times R-k}$. The choice of m should ensure that $X = k$ with great probability, and $P(X \geq m) \geq p_c$, with p_c close to 1, is called the confidence probability. Therefore, we choose m as the largest integer in $\sum_{k=m}^{R \times R \times R} P(X = k) \geq p_c$. For example, in our experiments, we set $p_c = 0.95$. Therefore, as examples, for $R = 3$, we have $m = 14$ if $p = 0.1$.

Proof of Algorithm Validity. In statistics, a consistent estimator with smaller bias and variance is better than one without bias but larger variance. Inspired by this fact, we would prove through two aspects (bias and variance of an estimator) that our method can ensure the small bias and variance of the $\hat{v}(i)$, an estimator of $u(i)$. Firstly, according to the *Law of Large Numbers*, we can draw the expectation of $\hat{v}^2(i) - u^2(i)$ as $E_i = E(\hat{v}^2(i) - u^2(i)) = \sum_j \frac{w_j}{w}(u^2(j) - u^2(i))$, with the number of noisy pixels n increasing unlimited, The E_i will be small when $x_1 \leq x_2 \leq \cdots \leq x_t$ and $w_t \leq w_{t-1} \leq \cdots \leq w_1$, where x_j is the absolute value of $u^2(j) - u^2(i)$. Actually, changing on these two orders would trigger the increase of E_i. To maintain these orders, it is necessary to find a strategy that can describe the similarity of $u(i)$ and $u(j)$ well. Secondly, we would consider the $D(\hat{v}^2(i))$, the variance of $\hat{v}^2(i)$, that can be written as $D(\hat{v}^2(i)) = \sum_j \frac{w_j^2}{w^2}\sigma^2$. According to the *Cauchy inequality*, we obtain the minimum of $D(\hat{v}^2(i))$ if and only if $w_1 = w_2 = w_3 = \cdots = w_m = \frac{1}{m}$, where m is the number of w_j that satisfies $w_j \neq 0$. $D(\hat{v}^2(i))$ is an increasing function of the difference between w_k and w_l, with $\forall k, l \in N_i(D)$. The above analysis and proof motivates us to find the most similar patches even with the accidental effect caused by noise interference. The larger the cubes are, the smaller the similar contingency is, which makes results more credible. Based on contextual analysis, we provide the rotationally and scaling invariant similarity measure to find more similar patches and then obtain the best estimation of $u(i)$.

Determination of Hyper-parameters.

3   Experiments and Discussion

Here, we report the results of several experiments to compare NMRSF with BM4DM, TriF, and Pri-NLM using a platform constructed by MATLAB 2015b

(MathWorks, USA) and Visual Studio 2012 (Microsoft, USA). PSNR and SSIM were used to measure the quality of images restored using different methods. Our experiments were done on synthetic data and clinical data separately. The synthetic MRIs (T1, T2) with 1-mm^3 voxel resolution (8-bit quantization) are from BrainWeb with different noise models (Rician+impulse) at different levels. The clinical data (DWI and DTI with 2.5-mm isotropic resolution) were downloaded from the DTI database, an *in vivo* human database, acquired under a Human Brain Project and National Research Resource Center grant.

Synthetic Data. The denoising results of one T1 weighted image and it's regional close-up views of each methods shown in Fig. 2 demonstrate the remarkable noise-removal and edge-preserving property of the RSNLM. In this case, we set $\Theta = \{7, 3, 358, 42, 0.4, 2\}$.

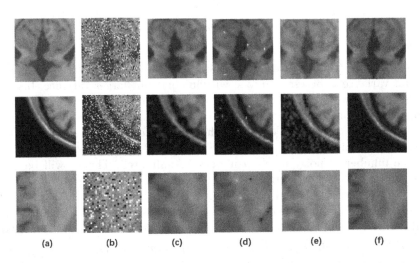

(a)   (b)   (c)   (d)   (e)   (f)

Fig. 2. Filtering results of an axial slice of T1 weighted Brain Web (Rician noise level of 5% and impulse noise level of p = 0.3). These three rows of images correspond to the results of three local parts respectively. Each column corresponds to (a) original image, (b) noisy image, result from (c) TriF, (d) Pri-NLM, (e) BM4DM and (f) RSNLM.

In Fig. 2, we can see the detail and texture of the cerebral cortex(line 2) and white matter(line 3) keeps better by our RSNLM than by the other method. As observed in Fig. 2(c) and (d), TriF and Pri-NLM removed most of the noise but impulse noise still remains, which blurred the image. BM4DM (in Fig. 2(e)) perform better than other two methods, but was still worse than RSNLM in preserving the boundary. Figure 3 shows the average of five sets of synthetic T1 weighted images denoising results(PSNR, SSIM). The denoising result indicates that the proposed method, RSNLM, outperforms the other method in terms of PSNR and SSIM values with different noise levels. The proposed method provided the best PSNR 34.9 with a SSIM of 92.3% for $p = 0.1$ and $\sigma = 3$.

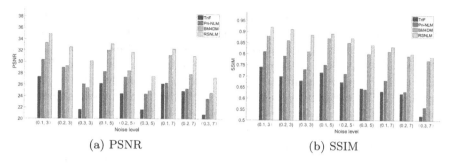

(a) PSNR   (b) SSIM

Fig. 3. The average results of PSNR (a) and SSIM (b) of five T1 weighted images with different noise level. "(A, B)" express the noise level with "A" for impulse noise and "B" for Rician noise on horizontal axis. From left to right different colors represent different methods with histograms, as follows (purple: TriF, blue: Pri-NLM, green: BM4DM and yellow: RSNLM) (Color figure online)

Compared with the second-best method, BM4DM, the average improvement is 2.59 in PSNR and 3% in SSIM, indicating that the high-level mixed noise can be satisfactorily removed by the RSNLM with edge preservation.

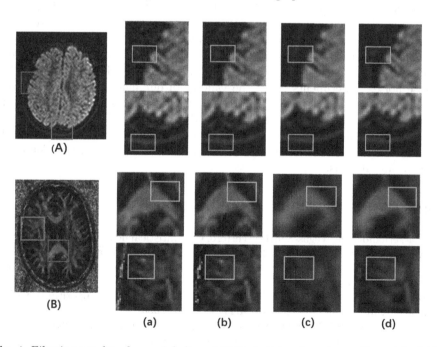

Fig. 4. Filtering results of an axial slice of DWI. Left-hand parts are the original (A) DWI and (B) DTI slice and its two local fields (red and blue), which are enlarged on the right. The first and second rows on the right-hand part are, respectively, the close-up view of the red and blue fields realized using different filtering methods: (a) TriF, (b) Pri-NLM, (c) BM4DM, and (d) RSNLM (Color figure online)

Clinical Data. We verify our method with clinical diffusion data(DWI and DTI) in Fig. 4. Compared with the experiments on synthetic data, the noise level of which is already known, an advanced automatic noise estimation method, PIESNO [7], is provided to estimate the noise level of special images. The proportion of abnormal points in the background is taken as the value of p. When performing DTI filtering, we consider the similarity of eigenvectors and eigenvalues of the diffusion matrix rather than the similarity based on pixels. The hyper-parameter set Θ is assigned as $\Theta = \{7, 3, 375, 13.5, 0.5, 4.5\}$ in the DTI image. In the case of filtering the DWI, the values of estimated σ and p are 27.5 and 0.093,respectively, with $\Theta = \{5, 3, 610, 21, 0.6, 2\}$. Just as is shown in Fig. 4, in the tensor field the BM4DM and RSNLM are also confirmed to be effective in preserving edges while removing noise. However, TriF and Pri-NLM blur structural boundaries, especially on the orange rectangle in the enlarged parts. A similar result comes from the fractional anisotropy (FA) of the DTI with four methods. The RSNLM reduces the ambiguity and unevenness of FA boundaries caused by noise more than BM4DM does.

4   Conclusion

In this paper, we propose a novel filter to remove the mixed noise from MRI images. We designed a new weight using the statistic $ROAD$ to detect the impulse noise and high-level noise. Ridge transformation (translation, rotation, and scaling) was used to obtain better neighbor similar patches. We also invoked the new adaptive parameter m estimation method depending on the level of impulse noise. Experiments prove the validity of our method against T1 data and diffusion data, such as DTI and DWI. Our method outperforms current state-of-the-art methods, such as TriF, Pri-NLM, and BM4D, not only in terms of recovered visualization but also in terms of data analysis of PSNR and SSIM. In the future, we plan to extend our method to other medical image denoising problems and models.

References

1. Aja-Fernández, S., Vegas-Sánchez-Ferrero, G.: Statistical noise models for MRI. In: Aja-Fernández, S., Vegas-Sánchez-Ferrero, G. (eds.) Statistical Analysis of Noise in MRI, pp. 31–71. Springer, Cham (2016). https://doi.org/10.1007/978-3-319-39934-8_3
2. Buades, A., Coll, B., Morel, J.M.: A review of image denoising algorithms, with a new one. Multiscale Model SIAM **4**(2), 490–530 (2006)
3. Chen, G., Wu, Y., Shen, D., Yap, P.-T.: XQ-NLM: denoising diffusion MRI data via x-q space non-local patch matching. In: Ourselin, S., Joskowicz, L., Sabuncu, M.R., Unal, G., Wells, W. (eds.) MICCAI 2016. LNCS, vol. 9902, pp. 587–595. Springer, Cham (2016). https://doi.org/10.1007/978-3-319-46726-9_68
4. Coupé, P., Yger, P., Prima, S., Hellier, P., Kervrann, C., Barillot, C.: An optimized blockwise nonlocal means denoising filter for 3D magnetic resonance images. IEEE Trans. Med. Imaging **27**(4), 425–441 (2008)

5. Hu, H., Li, B., Liu, Q.: Removing mixture of Gaussian and impulse noise by patch-based weighted means. J. Sci. Comput. **67**(1), 103–129 (2016)
6. Jin, K.H., Um, J.Y., Lee, D., Lee, J., Park, S., Ye, J.C.: MRI artifact correction using sparse+ low-rank decomposition of annihilating filter-based hankel matrix. Magnet. Reson. Med. **78**(1), 327–340 (2017)
7. Özarslan, E., Koay, C.G., Pierpaoli, C.: Probabilistic identification and estimation of noise (PIESNO): a self-consistent approach and its applications in MRI. J. Magn. Reson. **199**(1), 94–103 (2009)
8. Lin, C.H., Tsai, J.S., Chiu, C.T.: Switching bilateral filter with a texture/noise detector for universal noise removal. IEEE Image Process **19**(9), 2307–2320 (2010)
9. Maggioni, M., Katkovnik, V., Egiazarian, K., Foi, A.: Nonlocal transform domain filter for volumetric data denoising and reconstruction. IEEE Trans. Image Process. **22**(1), 119–133 (2013)
10. Manjón, J., Coupé, P., Buades, A., Collins, D.L., Robles, M.: New methods for MRI denoising based on sparseness and self-similarity. Med. Image Anal. **16**(1), 18–27 (2012)
11. Patz, S.: The Rician distribution of noisy MRI data. Magn. Reson. Med. **34**(6), 910–914 (1995)
12. Tomasi, C., Manduchi, R.: Bilateral filtering for gray and color images. In: ICCV, pp. 839–846 (1998)
13. Wiest-Daesslé, N., Prima, S., Coupé, P., Morrissey, S.P., Barillot, C.: Rician noise removal by non-local means filtering for low signal-to-noise ratio MRI: applications to DT-MRI. MICCAI **11**(2), 171–179 (2008)

Autism Spectrum Disorders (ASD) Characterization in Children by Decomposing MRI Brain Regions with Zernike Moments

Nicolás Múnera[1,2], Javier Almeida[1,2], Charlems Álvarez[1], Nelson Velasco[1,2], and Eduardo Romero[1(✉)]

[1] Computer Imaging and Medical Applications Laboratory - CIM@LAB, Universidad Nacional de Colombia, Bogotá, Colombia
edromero@unal.edu.co
[2] GIDAM, Universidad Militar Nueva Granada, Bogotá, Colombia

Abstract. Autism Spectrum Disorder (ASD) is a complex neurological condition characterized by a triad of signs: stereotyped behaviors, verbal and non-verbal communication problems and troubles in social interaction. The scientific community has been interested on quantifying anatomical brain alterations of this disorder to correlate the clinical signs with brain tissue changes. This work presents a fully automatic method to find out brain differences between patients diagnosed with autism and control subjects. After pre-processing, a template (MNI152) is registered to each evaluated brain, obtaining a set of segmented regions. Each region is mapped into a 2D collage image which is decomposed by the Zernike Moments, obtaining magnitude and phase. These features are then used to train, region per region, a binary SVM classifier. The method was evaluated in a children population, aged from 6 to 12 years, from the public database Autism Brain Imaging Data Exchange. The AUC values for the most representative brain region were 77% for ABIDE I and 76% for ABIDE II, demonstrating the robustness of the method.

Keywords: ABIDE · Autism Spectrum Disorders · Brain tissue · MRI · Inferior temporal gyrus · Zernike moments

1 Introduction

ASD constitutes a group of neurological alterations that represents a wide variety of clinical expressions. About 1 in 59 children has been identified with ASD according to CDC's Autism and Developmental Disabilities Monitoring (ADDM) Network. The prevalence in children is higher in boys than in girls, in a proportion of 4 to 1 [2].

Although there exist a large number of syndromes related to autism, the diagnosis remains until now strictly clinical. A reliable diagnosis requires availability of therapists or physicians, resulting in a bottleneck that difficult early

© Springer Nature Switzerland AG 2019
N. Lepore et al. (Eds.): SaMBa 2018, LNCS 11379, pp. 42–53, 2019.
https://doi.org/10.1007/978-3-030-13835-6_6

detection of this disorder [14]. In addition, most of early signs of brain function alteration are not specific and autistic signs may be observed in patients with no disorder, a source of confusion for many clinicians [31].

Currently, ASD diagnosis is performed using neuro-psychological tests that evaluate the patient-environment interaction and high cerebral functions. These tests register several clinician observations, making diagnosis subjective. The *gold standard* [12] in terms of diagnosis is the Autism Diagnostic Observation Schedule (ADOS) [24] and/or the Autism Diagnostic Interview (ADI-R) [25]. However the probability of misdiagnosis is high [15] since the clinician may mislead descriptive labels and inevitably introduces bias by her/his judgment [29]. Clinicians' experience may facilitate ASD diagnosis before the second year, yet the average diagnosis age is above 3 years, which suggests many children may not be diagnosed at all. Early ASD diagnosis is critical because earlier treatments can reduce the degree of deterioration and improve the function of both patients and carers [1]. Curiously, even if modern medical images are at the very base of many decisions, in these kind of pathologies their role is still marginal [36]. Neuro-imaging could be useful to evaluate relationship between the different areas, regions or set of cerebral regions and the cognitive and functional signs that patients present, that is to say, analysis of the structure offers new possibilities of correlating brain changes or alterations at the functional level with ASD signs.

Different researches have been done with the purpose of correlating functional alterations presented in ASD and the anatomical structures. The first approaches to this theory date back in 1991, when Kemper and Bauman analyzed brains of six autistic patients, finding main alterations at the level of the limbic system, cerebellum and inferior olive. These brains showed no major morphological changes, yet it was reported a decrease in the neuronal cell size and an increase of the neuronal density at the level of the amygdala and other limbic structures when comparing to controls [20]. Recent studies have used brain MRI to classify patients with ASD, resulting that main changes were in regions like the basal ganglia, corpus callosum, hippocampus, amygdala and thalamus [3,11,22]. Participants in this study aged 6–15 years, volunteer ASD and control subjects [18].

There is a strong ADS relationship with brain areas responsible for normal language development such as Broca's area and Wernicke's area at a level of verbal and non-verbal communication. There is evidence of increase in the volume of the right and left temporal gyrus in T1-MRI studies [5,16]. Other research has used more than three different classification techniques (RF, SVM and GBM) using as main feature the size of the cortical and sub-cortical regions, reporting a sensitivity of 57% and 64% of specificity for the binary classification task [19].

ASD characterization is difficult by the high variability between different medical studies and children development. An automatic morphometry approach has the advantage of including additional information to support early diagnosis, but some approaches based on voxel size, shape, or volume [30] ignore local and regional dependencies. A main contribution of the present research is a fully automatic morphometric method that establishes region differences by using local shape information. The approach starts by a brain segmentation using a known template [27]. Once the brain is segmented, each region is characterized by the magnitude and phase of the region Zernike Moments which inputs a standard classifier. Classification results using such feature space provide representative regions that differentiate between ASD patients and control subjects.

2   Methods

The proposed method is divided in five phases, as illustrated in Fig. 1, starting by firstly pre-processing each volume to eliminate differences coming from acquisition protocols and devices. Afterwards, an atlas [6] is elastically registered to each of the cases with the aim of segmenting brain regions. Each segmented region is then arranged in a two-dimensional collage of images, constructed by sequentially copying each slice into a 2D frame, from the top to the bottom of the region. The obtained 2D image is used as input to calculate the Zernike moments per region. The resultant magnitude and phase are used as features that are challenged to a classic classification task by means of a conventional Support Vector Machine (SVM).

2.1   Pre-processing

Each volume undergoes a pre-processing phase composed by two steps, first an intensity correction to reduce intra-site variability since images were not obtained by the same device and, second a brain extraction to remove skull, spinal cord and eye holes. Intensity correction was performed by the FSLMATH tool provided by the Oxford University [28], which corrects the bias field and normalizes each volume. Afterward, brain extraction was done by using BET (Brain Extraction Tool), which removes non-related brain tissues by using the histogram of the image and triangular tessellations [34].

2.2   Registration and Segmentation

The registration phase was carried out to obtain the corresponding regions from the Harvard-Oxford Atlas [26]. For so doing, the MNI152 template [27] was elastically registered to each brain. The process begins with an affine registration with 12 freedom degrees and a correction for spatial errors computed by means of the FLIRT Tool (FMRIB's Linear Image Registration Tool) [17]. Then, a finer result is obtained by performing elastic registration using the FNIRT [28] tool with a quadratic spline which optimizes the processing time and ensures that transformation is as accurate as possible.

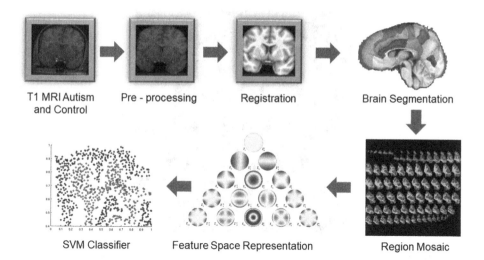

T1 MRI Autism   Pre - processing   Registration   Brain Segmentation
and Control

SVM Classifier   Feature Space Representation   Region Mosaic

Fig. 1. Pipeline of proposed strategy (1) pre-processing each volume, (2) a particular atlas is elastically registered to each case and the resultant volume is segmented to 117 regions, (3) each 3D region is mapped into a 2D-collage image, (4) the Zernike moments are computed per region, taking the magnitude and phase per moment as features, and (5) finally a classification task between ASD patients and control subjects to establish discriminative regions is performed.

2.3 Anatomic Region Representation and Collage

In the present work each segmented region, a volume structure, is represented as a 2D image that contains each axial plane. This collage is built by placing each slice in an squared resolution image, as seen in Fig. 2. However, note that each volume slice is fit to the size of the region, that is to say, while the volume resolution is 512×512, the resulting image resolution for a particular region slice could be 45×57. This representation is convenient because it allows to describe structural shape changes on each slice without any loss of information from the 3D original volume.

2.4 Region-Based Characterization: Zernike Moments

Zernike moments are considered as shape descriptors by performing a multiscale frequency analysis which is usually represented as a pyramid, where the scales are the different pyramid levels and frequency analysis (repetitions) is performed through each of the scales. The complex 2D Zernike moments of order m and n repetitions are defined in the unitary circle [23] as:

$$Z_{mn} = \frac{m+1}{\pi} \int_0^{2\pi} \int_0^1 f(r,\theta)V_{mn}^*(r,\theta)rdrd\theta, r \leq 1 \qquad (1)$$

where $f(r,\theta)$ stands for the image intensity function, $V_{mn}^*(r,\theta)$ corresponds to the complex conjugate of Zernike polynomial $V_{mn}(r,\theta)$, and m and n are both integers related as:

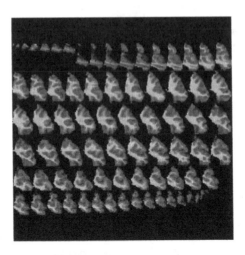

Fig. 2. An example of a 2D-image that represents a cortical brain region.

$$(m - |n|) \text{ is even and } |n| \leq m \tag{2}$$

For processing a 2D image, Zernike moments are computed by using the discretized form, as illustrated in Eq. 3:

$$Z_{mn} = \frac{m+1}{\pi} \sum_r \sum_\theta P(r,\theta) V^*_{mn}(r,\theta) \qquad r \leq 1 \tag{3}$$

In this work, a morphometric analysis was performed by transforming the 2D image into the Zernike space, a representation that has demonstrated describe complex shapes [23]. This representation allows to characterize each brain region based on shape differences between ASD patients and control subjects. Each brain region was described by using 9 scales (55 Zernike moments), where each moment consists of magnitude and phase components, obtaining at the end a descriptor of 110 features.

2.5 Classifier

Support Vector Machines (SVM) are a set of related methods for supervised learning, applicable to both classification and regression problems. A SVM classifier sets a maximum-margin hyperplane that lies in a transformed input space and splits the space, while maximizing the distance to the nearest sample examples. The parameters of the hyperplane solution are derived from a quadratic programming optimization problem [33]. For this investigation, the SVM algorithm was trained with the feature vectors obtained from previous phase.

3 Experiments and Results

The proposed strategy performance was evaluated by using a open access database [8]. The most important result is the identification of a set of brain regions that better differentiate the two classes, namely ASD patients and control subjects.

3.1 Database

For this study, brain T1-MRI cases were used, available in the *Autism Brain Imaging Data Exchange* ABIDE I and ABIDE II (first and second version) [7,8]. ABIDE databases contain 2226 cases (ASD individuals and typical controls aged 5–64 years), scanned across 17 medical centers. For this investigation, two subsamples were used, including only male cases with voxel size of $1 \times 1 \times 1$ and ages between 6 and 12 years, based on the criterion of growth and development of the cephalic mass in children up to 12.1 years [13], aiming to get an homogeneous population.

The evaluation was then carried out with 196 subjects (98 individuals diagnosed with ASD and 98 controls), 68 from ABIDE I database (Table 1) and 128 from ABIDE II database (Table 2).

Table 1. Strict sample phenotypic information for ABIDE I

Group	Age	Total	Mean	Standard deviation	Variance coefficient
Autism	6–12 years	34	10.88	1.87	16.94%
Control	6–12 years	34	10.96	1.75	15.77%

Table 2. Strict sample phenotypic information for ABIDE II

Group	Age	Total	Mean	Standard deviation	Variance coefficient
Autism	6–12 years	64	9.85	1.479	14.84%
Control	6–12 years	64	10.08	1.303	12.81%

3.2 Registration and Segmentation

The Harvard - Oxford atlas [26] was used as the reference space to segment each brain of the experimental group into 96 cortical (48 per hemisphere) and 17 sub-cortical regions. The lateralized template was rigidly and elastically registered to each brain, and the resultant transformation matrix was applied to the atlas parcellation, obtaining the set of brain regions per case. Registration was assessed by measuring the overlapping percentage (Dice Score coefficient [9] metrics) between both complete brain volumes, the registered MNI-152 and each case:

$$QS = \frac{2|X \cap Y|}{|X| + |Y|} \tag{4}$$

where: X is the MNI152 template and Y the evaluated brain. Once the elastic registration is performed, each brain is compared with the deformed template to verify that there is a high correspondence between the complete brain volumes. Registration results are shown in Tables 3 and 4 respectively.

Table 3. Overlap analysis for ABIDE I

Group	Analyzed cases	Register	Total overlap ± SD in %
Control	34	Affine	37.33 ± 6.02
		Elastic	97.62 ± 0.62
Autism	34	Affine	37.26 ± 4.58
		Elastic	97.54 ± 0.66

Table 4. Overlap analysis for ABIDE II

Group	Analyzed cases	Register	Total overlap ± SD in %
Control	64	Affine	30.51 ± 4.33
		Elastic	97.16 ± 0.91
Autism	64	Affine	33.43 ± 2.91
		Elastic	97.68 ± 0.30

3.3 Region-Based Characterization: Zernike Moments

In this phase of the proposed approach, there were computed 9 scales of the Zernike transformation, providing the first 55 moments of such representation space. This information corresponds to the shape orientations for each used region, and then magnitude and phase per calculated moment are concatenated on a matrix. Zernike moments were calculated the for the $n \times n$ 2D region mosaic-image described in the Sect. 2.3, using Matlab [32,35]. Figure 3 illustrates the complex parameters (magnitude and phase) provided by the Zernike moments for a particular region in the polar space.

3.4 Classifier

For evaluating the performance of the proposed approach by using a Support Vector Machine (SVM) classifier, a Radial Basis Function (RBF) was selected as kernel because of the high dimensionality of the feature vector per region. A 10-fold cross-validation scheme was used to train and test the constructed model, and four metrics are reported, namely Area Under the Curve (AUC), sensitivity, specificity and F-Score. It is noteworthy that the regions that showed greater accuracy were cortical regions, especially in those that are related to the normal language development, which play an important role in brain morphological

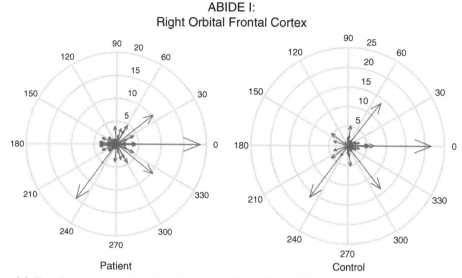

ABIDE I:
Right Orbital Frontal Cortex

Patient   Control

(a) Zernike representation for the region Right Orbital Frontal Cortex on ABIDE I

Fig. 3. Representation of complex parameters (magnitude and phase) for a cortical region (Right Frontal Orbital Cortex) provided by Zernike Moments. In (a) is presented the distribution of the complex values in a control subject and in (b) the distribution of the complex values in a autistic patient evaluated on the same region.

changes on autistic patients such as reported in previous researches [10]. Table 5 presents the classification results using the first 55 Zernike Moments for cortical brain regions.

Table 5. Classification performance for cortical and sub-cortical regions by testing with ABIDE I and ABIDE II. The reported metrics are: area under the curve (AUC), sensitivity (SENS), specificity (SPEC) and F-Score (F-S).

DATA	AUC	SENS	SPEC	F-S	Regions
ABIDE I	**77%**	71%	75%	74%	Left Supramarginal Gyrus, posterior division
					Right Frontal Orbital Cortex
					Right Intracalcarine Cortex
					Left Superior Parietal Lobule
					Right Thalamus
ABIDE II	**76%**	72%	72%	72%	Right Occipital Fusiform Cortex
					Right Lateral Occipital Cortex, superior division
					Left Lateral Occipital Cortex, superior division
					Left Lingual Gyrus
					Left Paracingulate Gyrus

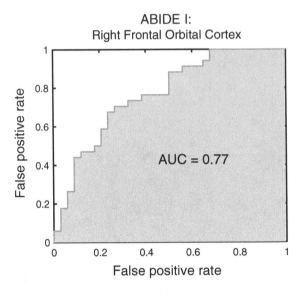

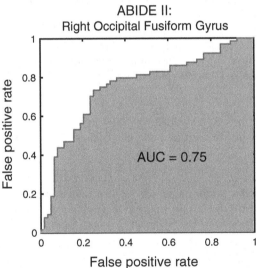

Fig. 4. Area under the curve for the most significant region per dataset, namely, ABIDE I and II.

Figure 4 shows the Area Under Curve (AUC) graph for the most significant brain region for ABIDE I (Right Frontal Orbital Cortex) and for ABIDE II (Right Occipital Fusiform Gyrus), found with Zernike Moments characterization.

4   Discussion

In the present study, we examined the orientations of the shape from each brain region using the Zernike Moments, in a large sample of children with ASD (Autism Spectrum Disorder), relative to TC (Typical Control). This representation does not find differences at the cellular level, but on the surface and how they are related to the abnormal growth of each region. Frontal Orbital Cortex is highly related to affective functions, decision-making and sensory integration [21]. It is possible to associate alterations in this structure with one of the signs present in autism related to communication and social interaction. [10].

Finally, we found associations with severity symptom within a thalamic surface area cluster. These findings suggest that there are subtle differences in subcortical morphology in ASD. Although this study was cross-sectional, our findings also suggest that there may be atypical developmental of intellectual function and performance deficits in ASD due to this atypical growth [4].

5   Conclusions and Future Work

This work presents a method for classifying patients diagnosed with ASD and how the anatomy of their brains differs from control subjects in particular regions. The variability of the disorder and the methods used by physicians for diagnosis is not completely reliable. The method used in this research works with high level features in MRI in order to represent the information as orientations in brain shape. The obtained results correspond to regions reported in state-of-the-art methods focused on image analysis based on other high level features. Cortical regions remain relevant in the study of autism due to anatomical variability of the brain, especially those related to the social interaction and communication. As a future work, we would like to make an inter-class classification to automatically determine the existing classes in autism spectrum disorder as Asperger, Classical Autism, Rett (present only in women) and other non-invasive developmental disorders described by the DSM-V guide.

Acknowledgments. This work is supported by INV-ING-2639 project, titled "Caracterización y cuantificación de anomalías estructurales en trastornos del espectro autista a través de imágenes de RM cerebrales (Fase II)", funded by the research vicerrectorate of Universidad Militar Nueva Granada at Bogotá, Colombia.

References

1. Alexeeff, S.E., et al.: Medical conditions in the first years of life associated with future diagnosis of ASD in children. J. Autism Dev. Disord. **47**(7), 2067–2079 (2017)
2. Baio, J., et al.: Prevalence of autism spectrum disorder among children aged 8 years-autism and developmental disabilities monitoring network, 11 sites, United States, 2014. MMWR Surveill Summ. **67**(6), 1 (2018)

3. Brambilla, P., Hardan, A., di Nemi, S.U., Perez, J., Soares, J.C., Barale, F.: Brain anatomy and development in autism: review of structural mri studies. Brain Res. Bull. **61**(6), 557–569 (2003)

4. Dager, S.R., et al.: Shape mapping of the hippocampus in young children with autism spectrum disorder. Am. J. Neuroradiol. **28**(4), 672–677 (2007)

5. De Fossé, L., et al.: Language-association cortex asymmetry in autism and specific language impairment. Ann. Neurol. **56**(6), 757–766 (2004)

6. Desikan, R.S., et al.: An automated labeling system for subdividing the human cerebral cortex on MRI scans into gyral based regions of interest. Neuroimage **31**(3), 968–980 (2006)

7. Di Martino, A., et al.: Enhancing studies of the connectome in autism using the autism brain imaging data exchange II. Sci. Data **4**, 170010 (2017)

8. Di Martino, A., et al.: The autism brain imaging data exchange: towards a large-scale evaluation of the intrinsic brain architecture in autism. Mol. Psychiatry **19**(6), 659–667 (2014)

9. Dice, L.R.: Measures of the amount of ecologic association between species. Ecology **26**(3), 297–302 (1945)

10. Dichter, G.S., Felder, J.N., Bodfish, J.W.: Autism is characterized by dorsal anterior cingulate hyperactivation during social target detection. Soc. Cogn. Affect. Neurosci. **4**(3), 215–226 (2009)

11. Ecker, C., et al.: Describing the brain in autism in five dimensions-magnetic resonance imaging-assisted diagnosis of autism spectrum disorder using a multiparameter classification approach. J. Neurosci. **30**(32), 10612–10623 (2010)

12. Falkmer T., Anderson K., F.M., C., H.: Diagnostic procedures in autism spectrum disorders: a systematic literature review. Eur. Child Adolesc. Psychiatry **22**(10), 329–340 (2013)

13. Giedd, J.N.: Structural magnetic resonance imaging of the adolescent brain. Ann. N. Y. Acad. Sci. **1021**(1), 77–85 (2004)

14. Ginn, N.C., Clionsky, L.N., Eyberg, S.M., Warner-Metzger, C., Abner, J.P.: Child-directed interaction training for young children with autism spectrum disorders: parent and child outcomes. J. Clin. Child Adolesc. Psychol. **46**(1), 101–109 (2017)

15. Hedley, D., Brewer, N., Nevill, R., Uljarević, M., Butter, E., Mulick, J.A.: The relationship between clinicians' confidence and accuracy, and the influence of child characteristics, in the screening of autism spectrum disorder. J. Autism Dev. Disord. **46**(7), 2340–2348 (2016)

16. Herbert, M.R., et al.: Abnormal asymmetry in language association cortex in autism. Ann. Neurol. **52**(5), 588–596 (2002)

17. Jenkinson, M., Bannister, P., Brady, M., Smith, S.: Improved optimisation for the robust and accurate linear registration and motion correction of brain images. NeuroImage **17**(2), 825–841 (2002)

18. Jiao, Y., Chen, R., Ke, X., Chu, K., Lu, Z., Herskovits, E.H.: Predictive models of autism spectrum disorder based on brain regional cortical thickness. Neuroimage. **50**(2), 589–599 (2010)

19. Katuwal, G.J., Cahill, N.D., Baum, S.A., Michael, A.M.: The predictive power of structural MRI in autism diagnosis. In: 2015 37th Annual International Conference of the IEEE Engineering in Medicine and Biology Society (EMBC), pp. 4270–4273, August 2015. https://doi.org/10.1109/EMBC.2015.7319338

20. Kemper, T.L., Bauman, M.L.: The contribution of neuropathologic studies to the understanding of autism. Neurol. Clin. **11**(1), 175–187 (1993)

21. Kringelbach, M.L.: The human orbitofrontal cortex: linking reward to hedonic experience. Nat. Rev. Neurosci. **6**(9), 691 (2005)

22. Lauvin, M.A., et al.: Functional morphological imaging of autism spectrum disorders: current position and theories proposed. Diagn. Interv. Imaging **93**(3), 139–147 (2012). http://www.sciencedirect.com/science/article/pii/S2211568412000587
23. Liu, M., He, Y., Ye, B.: Image Zernike moments shape feature evaluation based on image reconstruction. Geo-Spat. Inf. Sci. **10**(3), 191–195 (2007)
24. Lord, C., et al.: The autism diagnostic observation schedule-generic: a standard measure of social and communication deficits associated with the spectrum of autism. J. Autism Dev. Disord. **30**(3), 205–223 (2000)
25. Lord, C., Rutter, M., Le Couteur, A.: Autism diagnostic interview-revised: a revised version of a diagnostic interview for caregivers of individuals with possible pervasive developmental disorders. J. Autism Dev. Disord. **24**(5), 659–685 (1994)
26. Makris, N., et al.: Decreased volume of left and total anterior insular lobule in schizophrenia. Schizophr. Res. **83**(2), 155–171 (2006)
27. Mazziotta, J.C., Toga, A.W., Evans, A., Fox, P., Lancaster, J.: A probabilistic atlas of the human brain: theory and rationale for its development: the international consortium for brain mapping (ICBM). Neuroimage **2**(2), 89–101 (1995)
28. Woolrich, M.W.: Bayesian analysis of neuroimaging data in FSL. Neuroimaging **45**, S173–S186 (2009)
29. de la Paz, M.P., Arroyo, M.J.F., Aguilera, E.T., Muñoz, L.B.: Investigación epidemiológica en el autismo: una visión integradora. Revista de Neurología **40**(Suppl. 1), S191–S198 (2005)
30. Riddle, K., Cascio, C.J., Woodward, N.D.: Brain structure in autism: a voxel-based morphometry analysis of the autism brain imaging database exchange (ABIDE). Brain Imaging Behav. **11**, 1–11 (2016)
31. Rodríguez-Barrionuevo, A., Rodríguez-Vives, M.: Diagnóstico clínico del autismo. Revista de Neurología **34**(1), 72–77 (2002)
32. Saki, F., Tahmasbi, A., Soltanian-Zadeh, H., Shokouhi, S.B.: Fast opposite weight learning rules with application in breast cancer diagnosis. Comput. Biol. Med. **43**(1), 32–41 (2013)
33. Shmilovici, A.: Support vector machines. In: Maimon, O., Rokach, L. (eds.) Data Mining and Knowledge Discovery Handbook, pp. 231–247. Springer, Boston (2009). https://doi.org/10.1007/978-0-387-09823-4_12
34. Smith, S.M.: Fast robust automated brain extraction. Hum. Brain Mapp. **17**(3), 143–155 (2002)
35. Tahmasbi, A., Saki, F., Shokouhi, S.B.: Classification of benign and malignant masses based on Zernike moments. Comput. Biol. Med. **41**(8), 726–735 (2011)
36. Tomás-Vila, M.: Rendimiento del estudio diagnóstico del autismo. la aportación de la neuroimagen, las pruebas metabólicas y los estudios genéticos. Revista de neurología **38**(1), 15–20 (2004)

Digital Pathology

MP-IDB: The Malaria Parasite Image Database for Image Processing and Analysis

. Andrea Loddo[1]([envelope]) [iD], Cecilia Di Ruberto[1] [iD], Michel Kocher[2], and Guy Prod'Hom[3]

[1] Department of Mathematics and Computer Science, University of Cagliari, 09124 Cagliari, Italy
{andrea.loddo,dirubert}@unica.it
[2] Biomedical Imaging Group, École Polytechnique Fédérale de Lausanne (EPFL), Lausanne, Switzerland
michel.kocher@heig-vd.ch
[3] Institute of Microbiology, University of Lausanne and University Hospital Center, Lausanne, Switzerland
guy.prodhom@chuv.ch

Abstract. The visual analysis of peripheral blood samples is an important test for blood illnesses diagnosis, like leukaemia or malaria. Malaria is an epidemic health disease and a rapid, accurate diagnosis is necessary for proper intervention. Generally, pathologists visually examine blood stained slides for malaria diagnosis. Nevertheless, this kind of visual inspection is subjective, error-prone and time-consuming. In order to overcome these issues, numerous methods of automatic malaria diagnosis have been proposed so far. Unfortunately, no public image dataset is available to test and compare such algorithms. The aim of this paper is to present the first public dataset of blood samples afflicted by malaria, specifically designed to evaluate and compare algorithms for segmentation and classification of malaria parasite species. Every image is provided with its related ground truth and parasite's classification of type and stage of life. Our purpose is to offer a new comparative test tool to the image processing and pattern matching communities, in order to encourage and improve computer-aided malaria parasites analysis.

Keywords: Malaria · Red blood cells · Medical image analysis · Blood smear images

1 Introduction

Visual examination of peripheral blood samples is an important procedure performed by expert haematologists in order to analyse a pathology or to identify the patient's health condition. The manual analysis of blood smears is tedious, lengthy, repetitive and it suffers from the presence of a non-standard precision

© Springer Nature Switzerland AG 2019
N. Lepore et al. (Eds.): SaMBa 2018, LNCS 11379, pp. 57–65, 2019.
https://doi.org/10.1007/978-3-030-13835-6_7

because it depends on the operators' skill. The use of image processing techniques can help to analyse, count the cells in human blood and, at the same time, to provide useful and precise information about cells morphology. Peripheral blood smears analysis is a common and economical diagnosis technique by which expert pathologists may obtain health information about the patients. Moreover, blood cells images taken from a microscope could vary in their illumination and colouration conditions, as shown in Fig. 1.

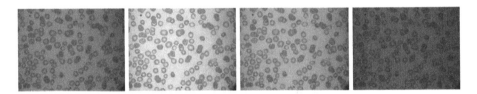

Fig. 1. Different illumination conditions could generate unconventional colour schemes in images. This is due to the absence of a standardized acquisition procedure. From left to right: same smear acquired with four microscope brightness levels. Courtesy of CHUV, Lausanne.

Typically, blood cells images contain three main components of interest: the platelets (or thrombocytes), the red blood cells (RBCs or erythrocytes) and the white blood cells (WBCs or leukocytes). It is worth considering that blood cells exist with different shapes, characteristics and colourations, according to their types. Many tests are designed to determine the number of erythrocytes and leukocytes in the blood (Complete Blood Count or CBC), together with the volume, sedimentation rate, and haemoglobin concentration of the red blood cells (blood count). In addition, certain tests are used to classify blood according to specific red blood cell antigens or blood groups. There are different calculations included in the CBC: number of red blood cells (red blood cell count, RBCC) or white blood cells (white blood cell count, WBCC) in a cubic millimetre (mm^3) of blood, a differential white blood cell count, a haemoglobin assay, a hematocrit, calculations of red cell volume, and a platelet count. Human malaria infection is not strongly related to cell count, but it needs different tests in order to be identified. It can only be caused by parasitic protozoans belonging to the Plasmodium type. The parasites are spread to people through the bites of infected female Anopheles mosquitoes, called "malaria vectors". There are five parasite species that cause malaria in humans and two of these species, Plasmodium Falciparum and Plasmodium Vivax, constitute the greatest threat. Plasmodium Ovale, Plasmodium Malariae and Plasmodium Knowlesi are the three remaining species that are less dangerous in humans [8]. Figure 2 schematically shows the morphologic and shape differences between the four acquired types and the related stages of life.

Computer vision techniques for malaria diagnosis and recognition represent a relatively new area for early malaria detection and, in general, for medical

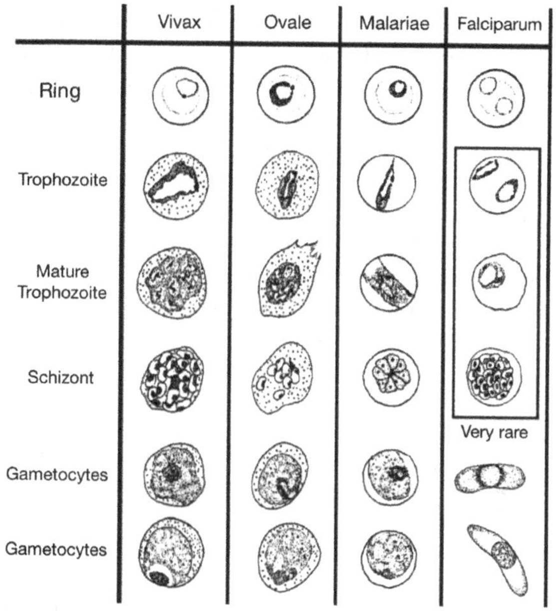

Fig. 2. Morphological scheme of human malaria parasites types and stages of life. Courtesy of Doc. Guy Prod'Hom, CHUV, Lausanne.

imaging, able to overcome the problems related to manual analysis, which is performed by human visual examination of blood smears [5]. The whole process requires an ability to differentiate between non-parasitic stained components/bodies (e.g., red blood cells, white blood cells, platelets, and artefacts) and the malarial parasites using visual information. If the blood sample is diagnosed as positive (i.e., parasites present), an additional capability of differentiating species and life-stages (i.e., identification) is required to specify the infection. Numerous methods of automatic malaria diagnosis have been proposed so far, in order to overcome the issues before mentioned. This kind of diagnosis uses images extracted from blood smears pictures taken by the microscope, after a staining process performed on the smears. Two main factors are generally considered if we refer to staining techniques: the type of colouration, in which Giemsa and Leishman are the most common, and the thickness of blood slide, which may be thick or thin. Typically, thin smears permit the identification of specific parasitic stage and quantification of malaria parasites; on the other hand, thick smears are better if the target is to perform an initial identification of malaria infection using blood pathology. Some examples are shown in Fig. 3. Giemsa stained blood smear is considered in most of the analysed literatures, whereas the Leishman stain is considered in few studies. It is reported that the Leishman stain has more sensitivity for parasite detection than Giemsa [2] and is superior for visualization of red and white blood cell morphology [6]. On the contrary, Giemsa stain highlights both malaria parasites and white blood cells and, therefore, it is an additional issue to deal with. The Giemsa stain is a more costly and also time-consuming procedure than Leishman. Moreover, magnification of 100X by using an oil immersion objective is used for capturing microscopic images of thin blood smear for identification of specific parasites and their infected stage. Due to the laboratory availability, this dataset has been acquired only from thin blood smears coloured with Giemsa stain. The dataset is public and free available by contacting the main author. This paper is structured as follows. Section 2 offers a deep description about malaria parasites, their morphology and characteristic. Section 3 describes how the dataset has been organized, blood samples analysis, acquisition and staining procedure, the images characteristics and parasites classification. Conclusions are given in Sect. 4.

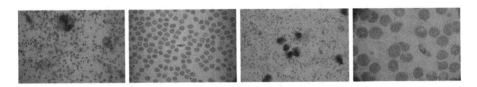

Fig. 3. Malaria infected blood smears types. This image shows a comparison between staining colouration procedures and smears thickness. From left to right: thick smear with Giemsa stain [6], thin smear with Giemsa stain [4], thick smear with Leishman stain [6], thin smear with Leishman stain [4]. Dots in thick smears and rings in thin smears are P. Falciparum ring stages, while elongated erythrocytes (in images on the right) are affected from P. Falciparum in its trophozoite schizont stage. The difference between thick and thin smears is clearly evident by observing cells and parasite shapes. Thin smears typically offer a better shape representation, while thick ones contain smaller and less clear region shapes. Furthermore, Giemsa stain shows a better contrast between cells, parasites and background respect to Leishman stain.

2   Parasite Morphology

A blood smear image, obtained through a microscope, is presented in Fig. 4. It typically contains at least three regions of interest: white blood cells (or leukocytes), red blood cells (or erythrocytes) and platelets (or thrombocytes). Two different categories of leukocytes exist: granulocytes (composed, in turn, of neutrophils, basophils and eosinophils). On the other hand, leukocytes without granules are called agranulocytes (composed of lymphocytes and monocytes). Erythrocytes do not have any subcategory even though malaria parasites (MPs) can infect them, consequently modifying their shape, morphology or colouration conditions. In particular, Fig. 5 shows several examples of malaria parasites in their different life stages and type. Although MPs infect only RBCs, a blood smear image representing both WBCs (particularly granulocytes) and MPs could be very difficult to analyse because of the similarities in colouration and shape between parasites and WBC grains, as shown in Fig. 4.

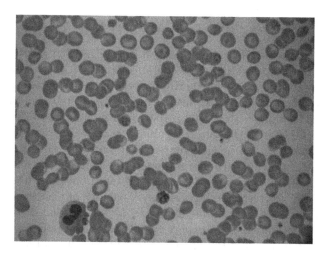

Fig. 4. Example of blood smear image acquired with a good colouration and illumination scheme. The image is characterized by three different regions of interest: a eosinophil granulocyte on bottom left, a schizont Plasmodium Falciparum on bottom centre and all the remaining cells are erythrocytes. Courtesy of CHUV, Lausanne.

MP-IDB collects four malaria parasite species: Plasmodium Falciparum, Ovale, Malariae and Vivax, in four different life-cycle stages: ring, trophozoite, schizont and gametocyte. It must be noted that Plasmodium Falciparum trophozoite and schizont are very rare and they are not present in our data collection. A complete set of examples, extracted from the dataset, are shown in Fig. 6. The life-cycle-stage of the parasite is defined by its morphology, size and the presence or absence of malarial pigment. The species differ in the changes of infected cell's shape, presence of some characteristic dots and the morphology of the parasite in some of the life-cycle-stages [7]. An automated malaria parasites analysis on blood smears usually comprises four different tasks, as follows:

1. Image preprocessing: the images are normalized in colouration, because it can differ a lot from image to image, and the different regions of interest are made the most contrasted possible.
2. Segmentation: red blood cells and/or parasites are separated from the background and white blood cells by using algorithms based on different characteristics of the cells (e.g. shape, colour, texture).
3. Feature extraction: relevant characteristic (e.g. shape, colour, texture) are extracted from the different region of interest in order to train an automatic parasite analyser.
4. Classification: several classification schemes can be performed. Hierarchically, cells are classified in red blood cells and white blood cells. Afterwards, red blood cells are classified in affected from parasite(s) or not. In the end, parasites are classified in their type and life stage. Parasites potentially can also be present outside the cells. In this case, they should need a more specific and dedicated analysis.

3   Dataset Description

Dataset images have been acquired with a Leica DM2000 optical laboratory microscope at Centre Hospitalier Universitaire Vaudois (CHUV) coupled with a built-in camera and software. The entire procedure has been realized under the supervision of expert radiologists, headed by Dr. Guy Prod'Hom. Every image is stored in PNG format with a 2592 × 1944 resolution and 24 bit colour depth. The images are taken with the same magnification of the microscope: 100×. This dataset is composed of 229 images, representing four different kinds of malaria parasite. Plasmodium Falciparum is present in 122 images, Malariae in 37, Ovale in 29 and Vivax in 46. Each image contains, at least, one parasite. Our dataset can be used either for testing segmentation capability of algorithms or classification system methods. It contains about 48000 blood cells, in which malaria parasites have been labelled by expert radiologists. The number of candidate parasites present in the MP-IDB is equal to 840. Specific counting, per parasite type and stage of life, is shown in Table 1. The annotation of the dataset images is described as follows. The image filenames are named with the following

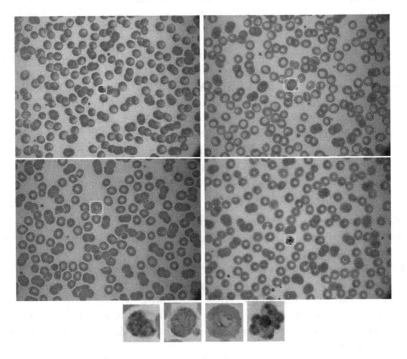

Fig. 5. Types of malaria parasites: from top left, clockwise, *P. Falciparum* in its schizont stage, *P. Vivax* in a gametocytes specimen, *P. Malariae* in its schizont stage, *P. Ovale* in its ring stage. All parasites have been surrounded with a yellow box. Underneath, from left to right: crops of P. Falciparum schizont, P. Vivax gametocyte, P. Ovale ring and P. Malariae schizont, taken from the boxes. Courtesy of CHUV, Lausanne. (Color figure online)

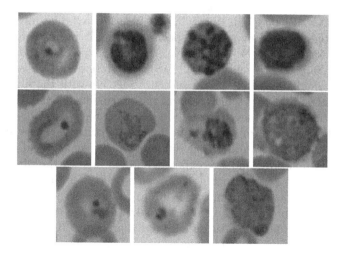

Fig. 6. Examples of malaria parasite stages. From top left: P. falciparum ring, trophozoite, schizont, gametocyte; P. ovale ring, trophozoite, schizont, gametocyte; P. vivax ring, developed trophozoite, gametocyte [4].

Table 1. Composition of dataset's images

Dataset properties		
Parasite (images)	Stage of life	Quantity
P. Falciparum (122)	Ring	695
	Trophozoite	2
	Schizont	20
	Gametocyte	3
P. Vivax (41)	Ring	9
	Trophozoite	27
	Schizont	1
	Gametocyte	10
P. Ovale (29)	Ring	13
	Trophozoite	11
	Schizont	1
	Gametocyte	8
P. Malariae (37)	Ring	1
	Trophozoite	18
	Schizont	10
	Gametocyte	11

notation: "ImXXXPR.png", in which "XXX" identifies a 3-digit integer counter, P represents one of the four parasite species ('F' for P. Falciparum, 'M' for P. Malariae, 'O' for P. Ovale, 'V' for P. Vivax), while the final R stands for the life stage ('R' for ring, 'S' for schizont, 'T' for trophozoite and 'G' for gametocyte stage). Every single image file has a reference text file with the filename notation set to "ImXXXC.xyc", which reports the coordinates of the parasites centroids. In particular, they have manually been estimated by a skilled radiologist at CHUV. These dataset images have been acquired with the same microscope. Unfortunately, lots of them suffer from different issues, like a typical non-uniform background illuminations and overexposed borders, due to the illumination of the microscope lamp (visible in Fig. 1). It causes also that the regions of interest can have different colouration, also due to the age of the analysed smears. It justifies a strong pre-processing step to make the image conditions the most similar possible, in order to realize an automated procedure. In fact, even though the images still remain intelligible, classic segmentation methods, e.g. based on thresholding, can suffer of these issues.

4   Conclusion

In this paper, we have shown how malaria parasite analysis is currently performed and which are the principal issues to deal with. Moreover, we have proposed a public dataset of blood samples, specifically designed to evaluate and compare the performances in segmentation or classification of malaria parasites by computer vision techniques. Our aim in realizing MP-IDB is to offer a strong image processing dataset, specifically designed to help in encourage new studies about malaria image analysis under a fair comparative approach based on a common dataset, like what ALL-IDB [3] has offered for leukaemia detection and white blood cells analysis [1]. We strongly discourage the use of this dataset for different activities than the purpose of this initiative.

References

1. Di Ruberto, C., Loddo, A., Putzu, L.: A leucocytes count system from blood smear images: segmentation and counting of white blood cells based on learning by sampling. Mach. Vis. and Appl. **27**(8), 1151–1160 (2016)
2. Khan, N., Pervaz, H., Latif, A., Musharraf, A., Saniya: Unsupervised identification of malaria parasites using computer vision. In: Proceedings of the 2014 11th International Joint Conference on Computer Science and Software Engineering, pp. 263–267 (2014)
3. Labati, R.D., Piuri, V., Scotti, F.: All-IDB: the acute lymphoblastic leukemia image database for image processing. In: 18th IEEE International Conference on Image Processing, pp. 2045–2048, September 2011. https://doi.org/10.1109/ICIP. 2011.6115881
4. Loddo, A., Di Ruberto, C., Kocher, M.: Recent advances of malaria parasites detection systems based on mathematical morphology. Sensors **18**(2), 513 (2018)

5. Rosado, L., da Costa, J.M.C., Elias, D., Cardoso, J.S.: A review of automatic malaria parasites detection and segmentation in microscopic images. Anti-Infect. Agents **14**, 11–22 (2016)
6. Sathpathi, S., et al.: Comparing Leishman and Giemsa staining for the assessment of peripheral blood smear preparations in a malaria-endemic region in India. Malaria J. **13**(1), 512–516 (2014)
7. Somasekar, J.: Computer vision for malaria parasite classification in erythrocytes. Int. J. Comput. Sci. Eng. **3**(6), 2251–2256 (2011)
8. WHO: Malaria fact sheet December 2016. http://www.who.int/mediacentre/factsheets/fs094/en/ (2016). Accessed 06 Mar 2017

An Algorithm for Individual Intermediate Filament Tracking

Dmytro Kotsur[1]([✉]), Roman Yakobenchuk[1], Rudolf E. Leube[2],
Reinhard Windoffer[2], and Julian Mattes[3]

[1] Software Competence Center Hagenberg GmbH, Hagenberg, Austria
`dmytro.kotsur@scch.at`
[2] Institute of Molecular and Cellular Anatomy, RWTH Aachen University,
Aachen, Germany
`{rleube,rwindoffer}@ukaachen.de`
[3] MATTES Medical Imaging GmbH, Hagenberg, Austria
`julian.mattes@mattesmedical.at`

Abstract. In this paper we propose an algorithm for automatic tracking of individual intermediate filaments (IF), which form a highly branched network inside living cells. The algorithm is based on Stretching Open Active Contours (SOAC) combined with a novel method for processing the snake's open ends. The main element of our approach (Endpoint-Controlled Active Contours) is a newly introduced potential function, which is included into the snake's energy term forcing its end-points to coincide with the filament's end- or junction-points. The comparison of our method with similar tracking algorithms for the problem of IF tracking shows a significantly improved accuracy of the overall tracking.

Keywords: Active contour model · Snakes · Point tracking ·
Intermediate filaments · Cytoskeleton · Confocal microscopy

1 Introduction

Intermediate filaments are major cytoskeletal components of vertebrate cells. Their molecular composition varies depending on cell type, cellular function and the microenvironment. Typically, intermediate filaments form a filamentous network within the cell and are mechanically connected to neighbor cells. This network is a main contributor to the biomechanical properties of cells and tissues supporting processes such as wound healing and tumor cell invasion [7,9]. The topology of intermediate filament networks is highly different depending on the cell type, filament type and physiological conditions. The organization and dynamics of intermediate filaments can be best studied in living cells producing fluorescent intermediate filament protein reporters. However, an approach to classify and distinguish between different types of filament topologies is missing. A quantitative description of network's characteristics using manual labeling of the filament's trajectories would be extremely time-consuming. Automated

© Springer Nature Switzerland AG 2019
N. Lepore et al. (Eds.): SaMBa 2018, LNCS 11379, pp. 66–74, 2019.
https://doi.org/10.1007/978-3-030-13835-6_8

filament tracking or segmentation algorithms have been successfully proposed for individual actin filaments which were well separated by background [8, 10]. The task of filament tracking within their highly branched network, in contrast, leads to additional complications due to a high spatio-temporal variability in the contrast of filaments and the risk of confusion with neighboring filaments. As an experimental evaluation shows (see Sect. 4), SOAC-based algorithms tend to overgrow or switch to the neighboring filaments.

In this paper, we introduce a new potential function to the snake's energy term. This potential function enables better control over the snake's endpoints preventing the issues with SOAC-based methods. After providing a scheme of the overall tracking procedure in the following subsection and describing the image processing steps in Sect. 2 we present our novel snake-based approach in Sect. 3. An evaluation on microscopic image data and a comparison to other tracking approaches is presented in Sect. 4 before concluding in Sect. 5.

Overall Tracking Algorithm. Our procedure for tracking of individual cytoskeletal filaments consists of two main steps: (1) fitting the filament's position to the image of the current frame and (2) transferring the filament's curve to the next frame in the sequence. For the second step, we use pyramidal Lucas-Kanade optical flow [2]. It allows to roughly estimate the filament's position in case of large deformations. Mapping errors are eliminated further on by the repetition of the snakes-based fitting step. In detail, the tracking algorithm consists of the following single steps (see Fig. 1):

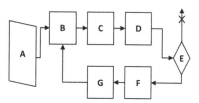

Fig. 1. Block-diagram of the overall tracking algorithm

(A) *Initialization*: The filament's position is initialized on the first frame (manually by the user or using an additional segmentation procedure [12]). The endpoint control term is initialized as described in Sect. 3.2;

(B) *Image processing* of the current frame according to the workflow described in Sect. 2;

(C) *Gradient vector flow (GVF)*: It is computed from the enhanced image (step (B), for details see step 2 in Sect. 2);

(D) *Endpoint Controlled Snake Evolution*: The snake is fitted to the current image based on the GVF obtained in (C) using a stretching [8] and an endpoint control term as described in Sect. 3.2;

(E) *Conditional Statement*: If the current image is the last in the sequence, terminate the algorithm, else go to the next step;

(F) *Pyramidal optical flow*: It is calculated for the current image with respect to the next one in the time-sequence as described in [2];

(G) Select the next image of the sequence, transfer the snake to it based on the calculated optical flow field. Update the endpoint control term as described in Sect. 3.2 and repeat the whole procedure starting from step (B).

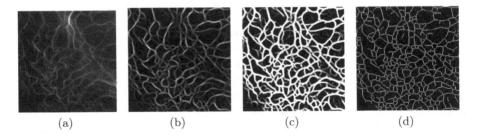

(a)   (b)   (c)   (d)

Fig. 2. The main image processing steps: (a) original image; (b) Frangi filter and gamma correction; (c) Thresholding using Otsu; (d) Skeletonization and junction- or endpoints detection (Color figure online)

2   Image Processing

Image processing of confocal microscopy videos showing intermediate filament networks should suppress noise, homogenize the highly variable intensity distribution along the filament's length and enhance the contrast of a filament. Intermediate filaments have a tubular network structure similar to a blood vessel tree but with a higher branchness and a lower variability in radius. In [5] it was shown that image processing algorithms used for vessels' contrast enhancement and segmentation can be adapted to confocal images of intermediate filaments. For every image of the sequence of N confocal images, we apply the following image processing steps based on the workflow proposed by [1]:

(1) Firstly, the original grayscale image (see Fig. 2(a)) is inverted and smoothed with a Gaussian kernel ($\sigma \approx 0.5$); the contrast of the image is enhanced with the CLAHE algorithm [1];

(2) the Hessian-based ridge enhancement filter by Frangi et al. [3] is applied in order to enhance tubular structures and suppress blobs and image noise. The contrast of the filtered image is further enhanced using gamma correction (with $\gamma \approx 0.5$) (cf., Fig. 2(b) for an example).

(3) Otsu's threshold T_{Otsu} is computed [1] and the image $I(x, y)$ is transformed using Otsu as an upper threshold: $I_{new}(x, y) = T_{Otsu}$, for $I(x, y) \geq T_{Otsu}$. The intensity range of the image is rescaled to $[0, 1]$ (see Fig. 2(c));

(4) A threshold value (≈ 0.25) is fixed in order to obtain a binary image;

(5) Noisy components of the binary image (with small area) are removed and a skeleton of the binary image is computed (Fig. 2(d)). Finally, the hit-and-miss morphological transform is used to detect branching/endpoints of the binary skeleton (see red points in Fig. 2(d)).

$$C_1(p) \qquad\qquad C_2(p) \qquad\qquad C_3(p) \qquad\qquad C_{total}(p)$$

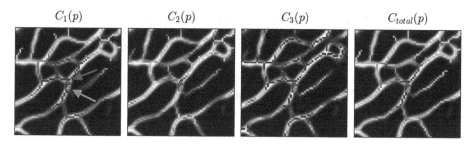

Fig. 3. Penalty function C_{total} and it's terms C_1, C_2 and C_3 computed for every point of the skeleton and encoded in color from blue for small values to red for large values. The green triangle represents p^{t-1} and the magenta one the bifurcation point p_b corresponding to p^t. Note that without $C_2(p)$ p^t might be wrongly selected as the next bifurcation below the green triangle. (Color figure online)

3 Filament Tracking Algorithm

3.1 Active Contour Models: Snakes

Let's denote by $\mathbf{x}^t(s) = [x(s), y(s)], s \in [0, 1]$ an open ended curve representing the filament's position on the image $I_t, t = \overline{0, N-1}$. We are fitting this curve to the current image by minimizing the following so-called "energy" functional [6]:

$$E = \int_0^1 \frac{1}{2}\big(\alpha|\mathbf{x}_s^t(s)|^2 + \beta|\mathbf{x}_{ss}^t(s)|^2\big) + E_{ext}\big(\mathbf{x}^t(s)\big)ds \qquad (1)$$

where α and β are parameters controlling the stretching and bending resistance of the curve, correspondingly. According to [6] we solve the following differential equation with an artificial time variable τ in order to obtain the minimum of the functional (1) above:

$$\mathbf{x}_\tau^t(s, \tau) = \alpha\mathbf{x}_{ss}^t(s, \tau) + \beta\mathbf{x}_{ssss}^t(s, \tau) - \nabla E_{ext}(\mathbf{x}^t(s, \tau)) \qquad (2)$$

In this case the "external energy" E_{ext} or the gradient of "external energy" ∇E_{ext} are computed based on the image data. ∇E_{ext} defines a structure within the image towards which the snake is converging.

Gradient Vector Flow (GVF). Xu et al. [11] are proposing to replace ∇E_{ext} by the vector field $\mathbf{v}(x, y)$, called gradient vector flow (GVF). The authors state that GVF is more robust and has a larger capture range in comparison with ∇E_{ext} defined in [6]. In our procedure we compute GVF based on the enhanced image obtained from the image processing step (3).

Stretching Open Active Contours (SOACs). Applying open-ended snakes as defined in [6] for individual filament tracking has the drawback that the snake tends to shrink over time. In [12] this issue is approached by using a stretching term for open ends $\nabla E_{str}(\mathbf{x}^t(s))$ in the ∇E_{ext} of Eq. (2).

3.2 Endpoint-Contolled Active Contours (ECAC)

In case of tracking intermediate filaments within their network SOACs tend to increase their length over time, grow beyond their actual position or even move into neighboring filaments. In this section we propose a method, which allows to avoid such undesired behavior by tracking the snake's endpoints independently.

Endpoint Control Term. Therefore, we define the following term E_{ends}, which allows to control the snake's endpoints and to prevent it from overgrowth. In the first analyzed image of the sequence we initialize a distance-based potential P as a sum of all RBF functions centered at the respective branching points p_b^0. These branching points are detected as described in Sect. 2, step (5). For every image I^t of the sequence we define two distance potential functions E_0^t and E_1^t corresponding to the two ends of any snake $\mathbf{x}^t(s)$. Initially, for I^0 we set $F_0^0 = E_1^0 = P$. For the next images $I_t : t > 0$ we define E_0^t and E_1^t separately. E_0^t (and equally E_1^t) is initialized by placing an RBF centered at a point p_*^t, which is the solution of the minimization problem described in the subsection "Endpoints tracking" below. Thus, we define E_{ends} based on E_0^t and E_1^t as follows:

$$E_{ends}(\mathbf{x}^t(s)) := \begin{cases} E_0^t(\mathbf{x}^t(s)), & \text{if } s = 0 \\ E_1^t(\mathbf{x}^t(s)), & \text{if } s = 1 \\ 0, & \text{if } 0 < s < 1 \end{cases} \tag{3}$$

The position of the snake on the current frame $\mathbf{x}^t(s)$ is optimized by solving Eq. (2), where ∇E_{ext} incorporates also E_{ends}:

$$\nabla E_{ext}(\mathbf{x}^t(s)) := \mathbf{v}(\mathbf{x}^t(s)) + \nabla E_{str}(\mathbf{x}^t(s)) + \nabla E_{ends}(\mathbf{x}^t(s)) \tag{4}$$

As a result, snake endpoints are captured by a force field and propelled towards their respective nearest detected junction- or endpoint on the skeleton.

Endpoints Tracking. Let's denote by p^{t-1} the position of the snake's endpoint on the image $t - 1$. In order to determine the position of the RBF center point p_*^t on the current frame we minimize the following cost function: $p_*^t = \arg\min_p C_{total}(p; p^{t-1})$, where p is a point sampled from the skeleton of the current image (image processing step (5)) in the neighborhood of point p^{t-1} in the previous frame. The total cost function is defined as a linear combination of three terms:

$$C_{total}(p; p^{t-1}) = C_1(p; p^{t-1}) + \gamma C_2(p; p^{t-1}) + \delta C_3(p) \tag{5}$$

where $\gamma \geq 0$ and $\delta \geq 0$ are weights balancing the contribution of each term. These three terms were designed to guide the tracking as follows (c.f., Fig. 3):

(1) $C_1(p; p^{t-1}) := \|p - p^{t-1}\|$ is a penalty for a large shift with respect to the position of p^{t-1};

(2) $C_2(p; p^{t-1}) := 1 - \langle \hat{I}^t_{p,s}, \hat{I}^{t-1}_{p^{t-1},s} \rangle$ is a penalty for local image pattern disparity based on the normalized cross correlation, where $\langle \cdot, \cdot \rangle$ is a binary operator defining zero-normalized cross-correlation of two images and $\hat{I}^t_{p,s}$ and $\hat{I}^{t-1}_{p^{t-1},s}$ denote image windows of size s centered at point p of the current image and at point p^{t-1} in the previous image, respectively.

(3) $C_3(p) := \min_{p^t_b} \|p - p^t_b\|$ is a penalty for a large distance to the detected branching points p^t_b on the current image (see step (5) of Sect. 2);

Finally, the distance-based potentials E^t_0 or E^t_1 are generated around the corresponding optimal solutions p^t_*.

4 Evaluation and Results

The tracker is initialized by interactively labelling the filament on the first frame and propagates it through the whole image sequence. On every frame of the image sequence except the first one we evaluate four distance measures between tracked filament and the ground truth filament.

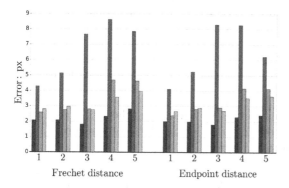 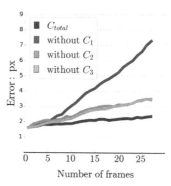

Fig. 4. Evaluation of the contribution of each penalty term to the tracking accuracy. The subfigure on the left shows the error distribution for the Frechet distance and the Endpoint distance for image sequences with IDs from 1 to 5. The subfigure on the right depicts the error accumulation over time. Thereby, the mean Frechet distance over all image sequences has been computed.

Ground Truth Annotation. In order to evaluate the intermediate filament tracking error we have produced a ground truth dataset comprising 5 sequences of confocal images.

The filaments selected for ground truth annotations were chosen randomly based on the criterion that a filament can be tracked visually by eye on every frame

Table 1. Ground truth dataset

Seq. ID	# Frames	# Annotations
1	27	100
2	50	100
3	50	50
4	50	50
5	50	50

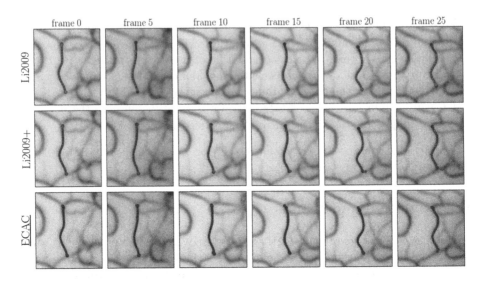

Fig. 5. Comparison of the tracking results for algorithms: "Li2009" [8], its modification "Li2009+" and our method (with endpoints control). The ground truth position of the filament is highlighted with a dark green thick line. (Color figure online)

of the image sequence. In total we obtained 350 ground truth filament trajectories. Short description of the dataset is shown in Table 1. More details: https://github.com/if-tracking/if-dataset

Distance Measures. We use four metrics for calculating the distance between two curves: Frechet distance, Endpoint (tip distance), Body distance, Length distance. The three latter measures have been defined in [4].

Evaluation Results. We selected the parameters α and β in Eq. (5) using a grid search on a training ground truth set. In order to illustrate the importance of each term of our penalty function C_{total} (Sect. 3.2) based on our distance measures, we evaluated our algorithm omitting one of these terms while applying the two others (cf., Fig. 4). Especially, when considering the accumulation of the error over time we observe that omitting only one term increases the error at least by the factor of 1.5.

We also compared our method (ECAC) to the filament tracking algorithm in [8] denoted here by "Li2009" and our modification of [8] denoted by "Li2009+" and described below. Both methods are based on SOAC combined with a Particle Filter (PF) for endpoint tracking. The main difference between "Li2009" and "Li2009+" is in the type of likelihood model $P_l(Z_t|X_t)$ used in PF. $P_l(Z_t|X_t)$ describes the probability of an image patch Z_t for a given position of an endpoint X_t. "Li2009" defines $P_l(Z_t|X_t)$ based on an appearance model (which according to [8] works well for tracking individual actin filaments). For the problem of IF tracking we modify (referred as "Li2009+") the likelihood model as follows: $P_l(Z_t|X_t = p) \propto exp\{-\mu \min_{p_b} \|p - p_b\|\}$, where the expression under the exponential is designed to take into account the branching points p_b^t in the current image and is equal to $-\mu C_3(p)$ (see Sect. 3.2). For our data we set $\mu = 0.5$.

As it's shown in Figs. 5 and 6, the combination of three penalty terms for endpoint tracking in ECAC significantly reduces the overall tracking error in terms of all defined measures and outperforms "Li2009" and "Li2009+". The described above modification of the likelihood model in "Li2009+" also boosts the performance of this algorithm comparing to the original model in "Li2009"'.

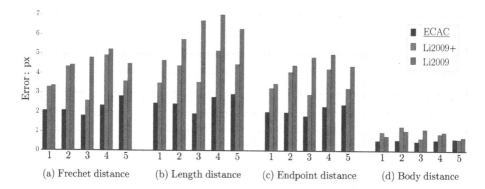

    (a) Frechet distance   (b) Length distance   (c) Endpoint distance   (d) Body distance

Fig. 6. Comparison of average errors of ECAC with the filament tracking algorithm "Li2009" and its modification "Li2009+" for each of the 5 image sequences.

5   Conclusion

We presented a novel robust snake-based approach called Endpoint-controlled active contours (ECAC) for tracking single intermediate filaments within their cytoskeletal network. Our approach outperforms state-of-the-art approaches for tracking cytoskeletal filaments by at least a factor of 1.5 in terms of mean Frechet distance reduction for each evaluated video. This allows to automate the analysis of geometric and dynamic properties of intermediate filaments over time and to characterize different filament populations within the same cell. In conclusion, the provided algorithm will help to understand how different architectures of intermediate filament network contribute to fundamental cell behavior.

Acknowledgements. The research received funding from the European Union's Horizon 2020 research and innovation program under the Marie Skłodowska-Curie grant agreement No. 642866. It was also supported by the Austrian Ministry for Transport, Innovation and Technology, the Federal Ministry of Science, Research and Economy, and the Province of Upper Austria in the frame of the COMET center SCCH and by the German Research Council (LE 566/18-2, WI 1731/8-2).

References

1. BahadarKhan, K., Khaliq, A.A., Shahid, M.: A morphological Hessian based approach for retinal blood vessels segmentation and denoising using region based Otsu thresholding. PLoS ONE **11**(7), 1–19 (2016)
2. Bouguet, J.Y.: Pyramidal implementation of the Lucas Kanade feature tracker: description of the algorithm. Technical report, Intel Corporation, Microprocessor Research Labs (2000)
3. Frangi, A.F., Niessen, W.J., Vincken, K.L., Viergever, M.A.: Multiscale vessel enhancement filtering. In: Wells, W.M., Colchester, A., Delp, S. (eds.) MICCAI 1998. LNCS, vol. 1496, pp. 130–137. Springer, Heidelberg (1998). https://doi.org/10.1007/BFb0056195
4. Gelasca, E.D., Obara, B., Fedorov, D.G., Kvilekval, K., Manjunath, B.S.: A biosegmentation benchmark for evaluation of bioimage analysis methods. BMC Bioinform. **10**, 368–368 (2008)
5. Herberich, G., Windoffer, R., Leube, R., Aach, T.: 3D segmentation of keratin intermediate filaments in confocal laser scanning microscopy. In: Annual International Conference of IEEE IMBS, pp. 7751–7754 (2011)
6. Kass, M., Witkin, A., Terzopoulos, D.: Snakes: active contour models. Int. J. Comput. Vis. **1**(4), 321–331 (1988)
7. Leube, R.E., Moch, M., Windoffer, R.: Intracellular motility of intermediate filaments. Cold Spring Harb. Perspect. Biol. **9**(6), a021980 (2017)
8. Li, H., Shen, T., Vavylonis, D., Huang, X.: Actin filament tracking based on particle filters and stretching open active contour models. In: Yang, G.-Z., Hawkes, D., Rueckert, D., Noble, A., Taylor, C. (eds.) MICCAI 2009. LNCS, vol. 5762, pp. 673–681. Springer, Heidelberg (2009). https://doi.org/10.1007/978-3-642-04271-3_82
9. Toivola, D.M., Boor, P., Alam, C., Strnad, P.: Keratins in health and disease. Curr. Opin. Cell Biol. **32**, 73–81 (2015)
10. Xiao, X., Geyer, V.F., Bowne-Anderson, H., Howard, J., Sbalzarini, I.F.: Automatic optimal filament segmentation with sub-pixel accuracy using generalized linear models and B-spline level-sets. Med. Image Anal. **32**, 157–172 (2016)
11. Xu, C., Prince, J.L.: Gradient vector flow: a new external force for snakes. In: IEEE Conference on Computer Vision and Pattern Recognition (1997)
12. Xu, T., Vavylonis, D., Huang, X.: 3D actin network centerline extraction with multiple active contours. Med. Image Anal. **18**(2), 272–284 (2014)

An Automatic Segmentation of Gland Nuclei in Gastric Cancer Based on Local and Contextual Information

Cristian Barrera[✉], Germán Corredor, Sunny Alfonso, Andrés Mosquera, and Eduardo Romero

CIM@LAB, Universidad Nacional de Colombia, Bogota, Colombia
{crbarrearm,gcorredorp,scalfonson,amosqueraz,edromero}@unal.edu.co

Abstract. Analysis of tubular glands plays an important role for gastric cancer diagnosis, grading, and prognosis; however, gland quantification is a highly subjective task, prone to error. Objective identification of glans might help clinicians for analysis and treatment planning. The visual characteristics of such glands suggest that information from nuclei and their context would be useful to characterize them. In this paper we present a new approach for segmentation of gland nuclei based on nuclear local and contextual (neighborhood) information. A Gradient-Boosted-Regression-Trees classifier is trained to distinguish between gland-nuclei and non-gland-nuclei. Validation was carried out using a dataset containing 45702 annotated nuclei from 90 1024×1024 fields of view extracted from gastric cancer whole slide images. A Deep Learning model was trained as a baseline. Results showed an accuracy and f-score 5.4% and 23.6% higher, respectively, with the presented framework than with the Deep Learning approach.

1 Introduction

Gastric cancer (GC) is among the most diagnosed cancers and the second most frequent cause of cancer-related death worldwide [1]. Geographically, the highest incidence of GC is in Asia, Latin America, and the Caribbean [2,3]. In Colombia, GC is the first cause of cancer-related death, representing a 15% of all cancer deaths, with a high incidence in the Andean zone, especially in the departments of Nariño, Boyacá, and Cundinamarca. Currently, it is considered a major public health problem that has generated an expense of more than 47 million USD in five years [4].

GC comprises several kinds of lesions with different severity grades. From such lesions, adenocarcinoma is the most common, representing more than 90% of all GC [5]. Characterization and quantification of the adenocarcinoma might establish plausible chains of events that improve the disease understanding and reduce its mortality rates. Diagnosis is usually reached by an endoscopic biopsy of the stomach which is processed and analyzed by pathologists who determine the degree of malignancy [6]. One of the most common approaches to identify

© Springer Nature Switzerland AG 2019
N. Lepore et al. (Eds.): SaMBa 2018, LNCS 11379, pp. 75–81, 2019.
https://doi.org/10.1007/978-3-030-13835-6_9

and grade gastric adenocarcinomas is by identifying and estimating the density of glands. Low-grade lesions are characterized by the presence of well/moderately differentiated glands (Fig. 1-a). In high-grade lesions, glands are highly irregular and poorly differentiated (Fig. 1-b) [5,7]. Identification of glands plays an important role not only in diagnosis but also in establishing some prognosis [7]. An accurate quantification is therefore essential for both the decision making flow and the treatment planning. Unfortunately, this process has remained highly subjective and prone to error. In this context, automatic measures may contribute to identify tubular glands on GC samples.

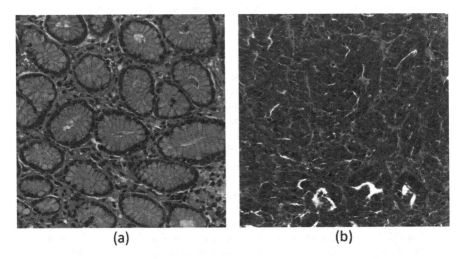

(a)   (b)

Fig. 1. Representative images of Hematoxylin-Eosin stained tissue from gastric lesions. (a) Well-differentiated glands, (b) Poorly-differentiated glands.

This work introduces an automatic strategy that exploits nuclear local and contextual information to identify gland nuclei in fields of view (FoVs) extracted from gastric cancer whole slide images (WSIs). The present approach starts by automatically segmenting nuclei with a watershed-based algorithm [8]. Each nucleus is then characterized by two types of features: first, its own morphological properties (size, shape, color, texture, etc.), second, its neighbor nuclei features within a determined radius. Such features are used to train a Gradient-Boosted-Regression-Trees (GBRT) classifier to differentiate between gland-nuclei and non-gland-nuclei. Unlike other state-of-the-art methods, any feature in this approach exploits nuclei relative information, i.e., any nucleus information is always relative to how such feature is with respect to its surrounding nuclei. This strategy is compared with a Deep Learning (DL) model that was trained to identify gland-nuclei. This DL model receives as input patches from WSIs and outputs probability maps that are thresholded. A watershed-based algorithm segments then the binary output map and splits the connected/overlaid cases to set the final candidates.

2   Methodology

2.1   Preprocessing: Nuclei Segmentation

A watershed-based algorithm [8] is applied to segment nuclei, generating a mask with the position of each nucleus. Each detected nucleus is then assigned to the class either gland-nucleus or non-gland-nucleus (See Fig. 2).

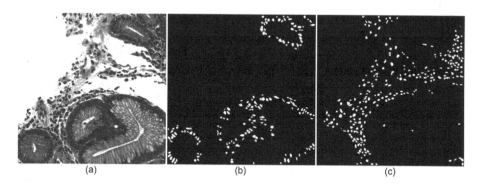

Fig. 2. Description of the nuclei segmentation. (a) Original image, (b) gland-nuclei mask, (c) non-gland-nuclei mask

2.2   Nuclear Local and Contextual Information (NLCI)

In H&E images, tubular gland nuclei are generally distinguished from other cell nuclei by their orientation, color, oval shape, eosinophilic cytoplasm, and proximity to other similar nuclei. For this reason, after nuclei were segmented, a set of low-level features were extracted, including shape (nuclei structural area, ratio between axes, etc.), texture (Haralick, entropy, etc.), and color (mean intensity, mean red, etc.). Each nucleus was represented by this set of local features. Additionally, for each nucleus, a set of circles with incremental radii of $k = dL \times 10$, $dL \times 20$, $dL \times 30$ pixels were placed at the nucleus center (begin $dL = 20$ pixels the averaged nuclei diameter), aiming to mimic a multi-scale representation. Finally, a set of regional features was computed within each circle and used to characterize each of the segmented nuclei. These features measure the neighborhood density and relative variations in color, shape, and texture.

A set of 57 local and contextual features were extracted from each image nuclei and the 33 most discriminating characteristics were selected by distribution analysis and Infinite Latent Feature Selection (ILFS) algorithm [9]. A GBRT classifier [10] was then trained to differentiate between the gland-nuclei and non-gland-nuclei classes. Specifically, we used an adapted GBRT framework [11] which emphasizes the minimization of the loss function.

2.3   Baseline

The baseline corresponded to a state-of-the-art deep learning approach known as Mask Region-based Convolutional Neural Network (R-CNN). This modification of the Fast R-CNN algorithm [12] has been used in the Kaggle 2018 Data Science Bowl challenge for identifying wider range of nuclei across varied conditions [13]. It uses a deep convolutional network with a single-stage training and a multi-scale object segmentation. Mask R-CNN outputs an object detection score and its corresponding mask [14].

The DL model was trained using a set of patches extracted from the FoVs. The positive class patches correspond to the area covered by the bounding box of each gland nucleus while the negative class patches were taken from the background, i.e., regions with non-gland nuclei. Aiming to increase the number of training samples, different transformations (e.g., rotation and mirroring) were applied to the patches. Model training was carried out using a total of 20 epoch cycles with 100 steps each.

Figure 3 presents the architecture of a trained DL model for the exploratory stage. A random extraction of a Region of Interest (RoI) is performed. This RoI is projected to a convolutional network that generates a feature map. These features are introduced to the RoI pooling layer for further processing. At the last stage, fully connected layers generate the desired outputs, including the gland nuclei candidate bounding box and mask.

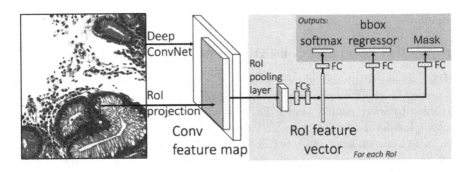

Fig. 3. Mask R-CNN work flow. Figure extracted and adapted from [12]

3   Experimentation

3.1   Dataset

The dataset consisted of 90 FoVs of 1024 × 1024 pixels at 40× extracted from a set of H&E WSIs taken from 5 patients who were diagnosed with GC. The WSIs were provided by the Pathology Department of Universidad Nacional de Colombia. A total of 45702 nuclei were manually annotated, being 12150 gland nuclei while the remaining 33552 corresponded to other structures (non-gland nuclei).

3.2   Experiments

Two experiments were carried out. The first attempted to classify between gland-nuclei and non-gland-nuclei using the NLCI approach. A Monte Carlo Cross validation method with 10 iterations was used. At each iteration, 70% of the whole set of FoVs was used to train the GBRT classifier and the remaining 30% was used to test the trained model. Finally, the measured performances along the 10 iterations were averaged.

The second experiment aimed to identify gland-nuclei using the DL model. For this purpose, 60 FoVs were used to train the model and the remaining 30 for testing. In this case, gland-nuclei detection was assessed based on the number of detected nuclei centroids that correctly overlapped with the ground truth nuclei, judged as correct when centroids were within one nuclear radius.

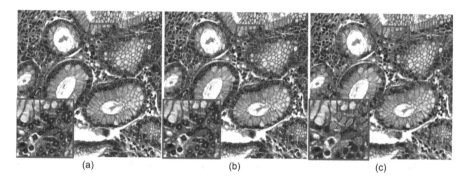

(a)   (b)   (c)

Fig. 4. Gland nuclei Segmentation showing, the ground-truth label (a), NLCI (b) and R-CNN with each gland nuclei candidate individually colored (c).

Table 1. Comparative measurements for both approaches.

Metrics	NLCI	R-CNN
Accuracy	0.977	0.923
Precision	0.959	0.585
F-score	0.955	0.719

3.3   Experimental Results

Table 1 presents different performance metrics for both assessed approaches. NLCI achieved an accuracy of 0.977 and an F-measure of 0.955, while R-CNN yielded corresponding accuracy and F-measures of 0.923 and 0.719, respectively. For the qualitative results, Fig. 4 shows the resulting gland nuclei segmentation from both approaches, where R-CNN generates its own masks of single gland nucleus presented by individual colors.

4   Concluding Remarks

In this article, two different approaches to automatically detect gland nuclei on gastric cancer images were presented and compared: a model based on nuclear local and contextual information and a DL model. Results demonstrate that local and contextual features are appropriate to describe the structural features of tubular gland nuclei. Despite the DL model presented good results, this approach requires a powerful/expensive infrastructure, long training times, and huge quantities of annotated data. Due to the lower precision of the model, it indicates the that only local information its taken into account. Future work includes quantification of glands to establish correlation with cancer grade and patient prognosis.

References

1. Hu, B., El Hajj, N., Sittler, S., et al.: Gastric cancer: classification, histology and application of molecular pathology. J. Gastrointes. Oncol. **3**(3), 251–261 (2012)
2. Karimi, P., Islami, F., Anandasabapathy, S., Freedman, N.D., Kamangar, F.: Gastric cancer: descriptive epidemiology, risk factors, screening, and prevention. Cancer Epidemiol Biomarkers Prev. **23**(5), 700–713 (2014). A publication of the American Association for Cancer Research, cosponsored by the American Society of Preventive Oncology
3. Ferlay, J., Soerjomataram, I., Ervik, M., et al.: Cancer incidence and mortality worldwide: Iarc cancerbase no. 11. http://globocan.iarc.fr (2013). Accessed 25 June 2018
4. Ministerio de Salud y Protección Social Instituto Nacional de Cancerología de Colombia: Plan Decenal para el Control de Cáncer en Colombia, 2012–2021 (2012)
5. Kumar, V., Abbas, A., Aster, J.: Robbins & Cotran Pathologic Basis of Disease. Robbins Pathology. Elsevier Health Sciences (2014)
6. Yoshida, H., Shimazu, T., Kiyuna, T., et al.: Automated histological classification of whole-slide images of gastric biopsy specimens. Gastric Cancer **21**(2), 249–257 (2018). https://doi.org/10.1007/s10120-017-0731-8
7. Martin, I.G., Dixon, M.F., Sue-Ling, H., Axon, A.T., Johnston, D.: Goseki histological grading of gastric Cancer is an important predictor of outcome. Gut **35**(6), 758–763 (1994)
8. Veta, M., van Diest, P.J., Kornegoor, R., et al.: Automatic nuclei segmentation in H&E stained breast cancer histopathology images. PLoS ONE **8**(7), (2013)
9. Roffo, G., Melzi, S., Castellani, U., Vinciarelli, A.: Infinite latent feature selection: a probabilistic latent graph-based ranking approach. In: International Conference on Computer Vision (ICCV) 2017, pp. 1407–1415 (2017)
10. Friedman, H.J.: Greedy function approximation: a gradient boosting machine. Ann. Stat. **29**(5), 1189–1232 (2001). https://www.jstor.org/stable/2699986
11. Becker, C., Rigamonti, R., Lepetit, V., Fua, P.: Supervised feature learning for curvilinear structure segmentation. In: Mori, K., Sakuma, I., Sato, Y., Barillot, C., Navab, N. (eds.) MICCAI 2013. LNCS, vol. 8149, pp. 526–533. Springer, Heidelberg (2013). https://doi.org/10.1007/978-3-642-40811-3_66

12. Girshick, R.: Fast R-CNN. In: ICCV 2015 (2015). https://arxiv.org/abs/1504.08083
13. Kaggle: 2018 data science bowl. Booz Allen Hamilton (2018). https://www.kaggle.com/c/data-science-bowl-2018
14. He, K., Gkioxari, G., Dollár, P., Girshick, R.: Mask R-CNN. Facebook AI Research (2017). https://arxiv.org/abs/1703.06870

A Transfer Learning Exploited for Indexing Protein Structures from 3D Point Clouds

Halim Benhabiles[1(✉)], Karim Hammoudi[2,3], Feryal Windal[1],
Mahmoud Melkemi[2,3], and Adnane Cabani[4]

[1] ISEN-Lille, Yncréa Hauts-de-France, Lille, France
{halim.benhabiles,feryal.windal}@yncrea.fr
[2] Department of Computer Science, IRIMAS, Université de Haute-Alsace,
68100 Mulhouse, France
[3] Université de Strasbourg, Strasbourg, France
{karim.hammoudi,mahmoud.melkemi}@uha.fr
[4] Normandie University, UNIROUEN, ESIGELEC, IRSEEM, 76000 Rouen, France
adnane.cabani@esigelec.fr

Abstract. In this paper, we propose a transfer learning-based methodology that can be exploited for indexing protein structures from associated 3D point clouds. Such a methodology can be particularly useful for biologists that are searching automated solutions to find family members of a query protein or even to label new structures by directly using input raw 3D point clouds. Comparative study and performance evaluation show the efficiency and the potential of the proposed methodology.

Keywords: Transfer learning · Protein structure analysis ·
Indexing 3D point clouds · PDB · Biomedical imaging

1 Introduction and Motivation

Identifying protein functions and analyzing their interactions can help to understand the mechanisms that govern the living beings, and accordingly, to establish new effective therapeutic strategies. In most cases, functions of a protein can be predicted through analysis of its structure, itself characterized by the composition of its molecules (e.g., amino acids) as well as their relationships and spatial positions [4].

In this sense, methods are used for separating proteins from their other cellular compounds (e.g., ultracentrifugation, electrophoresis). Then, their structures can be studied by varied methods such as X-ray crystallography, Nuclear Magnetic Resonance or mass spectrometer. Biologists and biochemists from around the world regularly exploit these analysis methods and submit their obtained data (e.g., 3D structural information of biological macromolecules) in a mutual and public database that is named Protein Data Bank (PDB[1]) [2].

---

[1] Guide to Understanding PDB Data: https://pdb101.rcsb.org/learn/guide-to-understanding-pdb-data/introduction.

© Springer Nature Switzerland AG 2019
N. Lepore et al. (Eds.): SaMBa 2018, LNCS 11379, pp. 82–89, 2019.
https://doi.org/10.1007/978-3-030-13835-6_10

Various bioinformatics research topics that have been investigated in the literature for analyzing proteins are presented hereafter.

Due to the increasing interest for the analysis of protein and to the development of emerging instruments and technologies, the size and the diversity of digitized protein information are more and more high *making then complex the exploitation for such a database*. In [5], a freely available web-based database exploration tool (PDB-Explorer[2] website) is proposed and permits to interactively visualize and explore the structural diversity of the PDB (e.g., through color-coded map generation or structure classification).

In [14], the author tackles the *problem of functional annotation* from protein 3D structures for which most solutions use 3D structure superposition techniques that are computationally demanding. The author combines geometry characteristics and physicochemical features for efficiently analyzing the protein surfaces.

In [7], the authors study the *problem of understanding protein-protein interactions*. They propose a methodology of predicting of Hot-Spots in protein-protein interfaces. The presented model is trained on a large number of structural and evolutionary sequence-based features. Also, several classification algorithms with cost functions are utilized. The best model is selected by using c-forest, a random forest ensemble learning method.

In this paper, our goal is to present a transfer learning-based methodology for indexing protein structures represented by 3D point clouds. Indeed, a neural network training process can be computationally time consuming. Additionally, it requires the preparation of ground-truths which is a fastidious task (manual data labelling). Hence, instead of training a neural network, a pre-trained one with generic 3D objects is directly exploited to characterise protein structures. Our proposed indexing methodology is important for biologists that are searching automated solutions to find family members of a query protein or even to label new structures by directly using input raw 3D point clouds.

2   Proposed Methodology

A transfer learning is an operation that consists of exploiting knowledge gained to solve a problem and applying it to solve a different but related problem. Nevertheless, efficient transfer learning needs surrounding processing stages for its adaptation to the targeted problem with respect to its applicative context. In this section, we describe the proposed methodology which is entitled "Generic Learning-based Transfer for Indexing Proteins (GLT4IP)". It is focused on a transfer learning-based indexing method for 3D protein shape retrieval.

Figure 1 provides an overview of the associated major stages. First, the input protein which is represented in the form of a 3D point cloud is resampled and normalized. The resulting pre-processed protein data is injected into a Convolutional Neural Network (CNN) through a classification architecture that was already pre-trained onto a 3D object database. Since this database was composed

---

[2] PDB-Explorer website: http://www.cheminfo.org/pdbexplorer/.

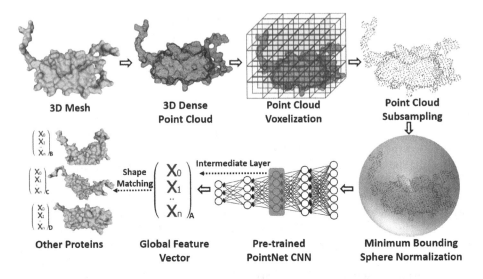

Fig. 1. Overview of our proposed transfer learning-based method.

of a large variety of man-made objects, it made data structures and parameters of the exploited CNN architecture (e.g., associated layers, weight coefficients) particularly tuned for classifying a large variety of object shapes. A transfer learning is then applied by extracting from this CNN architecture, for each protein, a feature vector that is globally embedding structural information of the protein with a generic manner. Finally, extracted protein feature vectors are used to compute the similarity scores from the ones to the others. A sorting of similarity scores can then permit to identify proteins having similar structural characteristics to a query protein—protein shape indexing.

2.1 Sub-sampling of the Considered Protein Point Clouds

Before to proceed to the feature extraction and in order to be able to exploit the considered CNN architecture, the 3D point cloud representing the protein surface (several thousand of points) is sub-sampled in order to reduce its size to 2048 3D points while keeping its global structure. This sub-sampling stage is done to adjust the protein data size to the size of input data that is managed by the CNN architecture. To this end, we apply a volumetric-based clustering algorithm on the original protein by exploiting a simplification method that was proposed in [1]. In particular, the minimum bounding box of the object is subdivided into a 3D voxel grid according to a leaf size parameter (voxel size). This latter parameter is set according to the targeted size of the final point cloud (2048 3D values). The resulting point cloud is then generated by calculating the centroids of the voxels containing points. The main advantage of such a transformation is its ability to preserve the global structure of the object thanks to a uniform sampling of the original surface. Additionally, it is known to be computationally fast thanks to the use of advanced data structures (see octree of the Point Cloud Library [11]).

2.2   Normalization of the Sub-sampled Protein Point Clouds

Once we obtained the sub-sampled point clouds, the next stage consists of their normalization in order to make coherent the targeted protein-to-protein comparison process. The applied normalization stage is twofold: (i) the sub-sampled 3D point clouds of proteins are spatially rescaled. To reach this goal, the object is normalized into a unit sphere corresponding to the minimal bounding sphere. This step is performed by using an algorithm which has the advantage of not being time consuming ([13] and [9]), (ii) each resulting rescaled 3D point cloud is then re-centered by computing its barycenter and by operating a zero-mean translation to its associated points (i.e. registration of the 3D points to a zero point of common XYZ referential). It is worth mentioning that the quantity of each normalized 3D protein point cloud has not changed and is still equal to 2048.

2.3   Extraction of Structural Feature Vectors

Each prepared protein 3D point cloud (natural 3D object) is then injected into a CNN architecture that was pretrained over a large database of diverse manmade 3D objects in order to benefit from a deep analyzer already calibrated with structural classification objectives (transfer learning). Indeed, deep learning architecture of these recent years are pushing the frontier of performance in many computer vision and 3D applications including data detection, segmentation and classification. Our methodology exploits the PointNet classification architecture [8] as a generic feature vector extractor.

More precisely, in our case we did not consider the output of the last layer of this architecture (i.e. classification vector). We use the pretrained network for extracting a global descriptor vector corresponding to an intermediate fully connected layer giving the best experimental performance. To reach this goal, we have conducted an empirical study to identify which layer level gives the highest performance (see the architecture layers in Fig. 2 of [8]). Consequently, the feature vectors that are generated for the prepared protein implicitly take advantage of information learned on a dataset of approximately 12,300 CAD 3D objects with 40 possible categories (details of operations and training protocols are presented in the PointNet reference).

2.4   Shape Matching

Having generated a descriptor vector for each protein, the last stage consists of measuring the protein-to-protein similarity. To this end, we experimented cost functions over the descriptor vectors, namely the Euclidean distance and the Earth Movers distance [10]. Proteins are sorted from the closest one to the

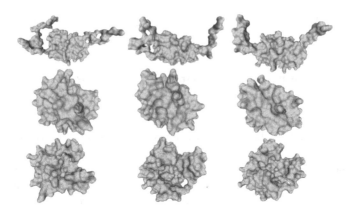

Fig. 2. On each row, examples of proteins belonging to the same class from SHREC2018 protein dataset.

furthest one with respect to each query protein (e.g.; for generating a distance matrix necessary to the object indexing). Both functions provide a dissimilarity score between two compared proteins and a 0 value output means that they are equal.

3   Experimental Results and Performance Evaluation

Our method has been experimented on the SHREC2018 protein dataset and compared to the related state-of-the-art methods [6]. The SHREC2018 protein dataset is composed of 2267 proteins. Each protein is represented by two formats, namely PDB and OFF which give a total number of 4534 files. As raised in the introduction, the PDB (Protein Data Bank) is the standard format that is used by the biologist community. This format describes the protein structure in the form of a point cloud where each point is the center of an atom. The OFF (Object File Format) format describes the surface of the protein in the form of a mesh of triangles. In this latter case, each atom is approximated by a sphere.

The 2267 proteins have been organized into 107 classes where each class represents a protein domain. The dataset has been built following a specific protocol while considering standard references including the protein structure database PDB [2] as well as the SCOPe database (Structural Classification Of Proteins - extended) [3]. For more details on the protocol followed to build the dataset, we refer the reader to the original paper [6]. Figure 2 illustrates some proteins in the OFF format. Each row shows examples of proteins belonging to the same class.

To evaluate the performance of our method, we considered the OFF files of the 2267 proteins. For each protein, we have applied the processing pipeline described in our methodology to extract the feature vectors. As stated previously in the paper, for the feature extraction stage, we employ a transfer learning from the PointNet [8] CNN classification architecture. This allowed to generate for each protein three feature vectors corresponding to three intermediate and successively fully connected layers for which the sizes are 1024, 512 and 256, respectively.

Figure 3 shows the precision-recall curves obtained by our method for the three feature vectors and using two different distances for the shape matching step: the Euclidean distance and the Earth Movers distance. For this later, we only display the best curve obtained among the three (the one based on a vector of size 1024) for clarity's sake. The figure clearly shows that the best retrieval results correspond to the ones calculated from feature vectors of size 1024 using Euclidean distance.

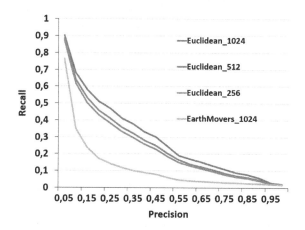

Fig. 3. Precision-recall curves obtained by our method with different settings.

Moreover, some other standard metrics [12] have been considered in our evaluation:

- Nearest Neighbor (NN): the percentage of objects belonging to the query class and ranked in the top k of the retrieval result where $k = 1$.
- First Tier (T1): the same idea as in NN where k depends on the size of the class query. If the class size is C then $k = C - 1$.
- Second Tier (T2): in this case $k = 2 * (C - 1)$.
- E-Measure (EM): the precision and recall calculated on the first 32 retrieved objects.
- Discounted Cumulative Gain (DCG): assuming that the user pays more attention on the first displayed results of a search, this measure assigns more weight to the relevant results located at the top of the list.

All these metrics are ranged in $[0, 1]$ where 1 indicates the best performance. Using these metrics, we compared our best results (Euclidean distance calculated on 1024 dimensional vectors) with some of the most recent methods having exploited the SHREC2018 protein dataset. More precisely, we compared our method (GLT4IP) with six methods described in [6]: 3D convolutional framework for protein shape retrieval (3D-FusionNet), Global Spectral Graph Wavelet framework (GSGW), Histograms of Area Projection Transform (HAPT), Protein Shape Retrieval driven by Digital Elevation Models (DEM), Scale-Invariant Wave Kernel Signature (SIWKS) and Wave Kernel Signature (WKS).

Table 1 summarizes the performances obtained by our method and by the six methods on the SHREC2018 protein dataset. It shows that our method GLT4IP reaches better results than GSGW, DEM and SIWKS. Three other methods outperform GLT4IP but this latter remains complementary since relatively fast outputs are obtained through the pre-trained CNN. Nevertheless, performances obtained by all current methods clearly show that characterizing the shapes of the proteins is not an obvious task, probably in reason of their high diversity and irregularity of shapes which make the current descriptors partially efficient.

Table 1. Performances of our proposed method GLT4IP compared to those of the state of the art methods obtained on the SHREC2018 protein dataset.

Method	NN	T1	T2	EM	DCG
GLT4IP	0.550	0.293	0.344	0.265	0.598
3D-FusionNet	0.689	0.404	0.459	0.366	0.681
GSGW	0.514	0.261	0.35	0.247	0.581
HAPT	0.77	0.493	0.584	0.462	0.755
DEM	0.421	0.238	0.319	0.231	0.555
SIWKS	0.199	0.109	0.189	0.114	0.452
WKS	0.717	0.41	0.49	0.377	0.701

4   Conclusion

The paper presents an approach (GLT4IP) indexing protein structures from associated 3D point clouds. The protein data is subsampled to fit with the input size of a CNN that was already pretrained onto man-made 3D object database. The subsampling stage is performed while keeping the shape topology. By subsampling data and transferring knowledge from a pretrained CNN, it makes GLT4IP relatively fast. GLT4IP performances overpass half of the state-of-the-art methods involved in the SHREC2018 contest. GLT4IP reveals the potential of a prepared transfer learning-based method for competing with research methods in protein shape retrieval.

Acknowledgments. The authors particularly thank F. Langenfeld, organizing member of the SCHREC 2018 challenge for his assistance and the double-check of the performance rates for our method presented in Table 1. They thank F. Malbranque, V. Tondeux, A. Jaffrezic and J. Xu for deploying the processing pipeline.

References

1. Benhabiles, H., Aubreton, O., Barki, H., Tabia, H.: Fast simplification with sharp feature preserving for 3D point clouds. In: 2013 11th International Symposium on Programming and Systems (ISPS), pp. 47–52, April 2013. https://doi.org/10.1109/ISPS.2013.6581492

2. Berman, H.M., et al.: The protein data bank. Nucleic Acids Res. **28**(1), 235–242 (2000). https://doi.org/10.1093/nar/28.1.235

3. Chandonia, J.M., Fox, N.K., Brenner, S.E.: SCOPe: manual curation and artifact removal in the structural classification of proteins extended database. J. Mol. Biol. **429**(3), 348–355 (2017). https://doi.org/10.1016/j.jmb.2016.11.023. Computation Resources for Molecular Biology

4. Hegyi, H., Gerstein, M.: The relationship between protein structure and function: a comprehensive survey with application to the yeast genome. J. Mol. Biol. **288**(1), 147–164 (1999). https://doi.org/10.1006/jmbi.1999.2661. Edited by G. von Heijne

5. Jin, X., Awale, M., Zasso, M., Kostro, D., Patiny, L., Reymond, J.L.: PDB-explorer: a web-based interactive map of the protein data bank in shape space. BMC Bioinform. **16**(1), 339 (2015). https://doi.org/10.1186/s12859-015-0776-9

6. Langenfeld, F., et al.: SHREC 2018 protein shape retrieval. In: Eurographics Workshop on 3D Object Retrieval, pp. 53–61, April 2018. https://doi.org/10.2312/3dor.20181053

7. Melo, R., et al.: A machine learning approach for hot-spot detection at protein-protein interfaces. Int. J. Mol. Sci. **17**(8) (2016). https://doi.org/10.3390/ijms17081215

8. Qi, C.R., Su, H., Mo, K., Guibas, L.J.: Pointnet: deep learning on point sets for 3D classification and segmentation. In: Proceedings of the Computer Vision and Pattern Recognition (CVPR). IEEE (2017)

9. Ritter, J.: An efficient bounding sphere. In: Graphics Gems, pp. 301–303. Academic Press Professional Inc., San Diego (1990)

10. Rubner, Y., Tomasi, C., Guibas, L.J.: A metric for distributions with applications to image databases. In: IEEE International Conference on Computer Vision, pp. 59–66, Bombay, India, 9–13 May 1998

11. Rusu, R.B., Cousins, S.: 3D is here: point cloud library (PCL). In: IEEE International Conference on Robotics and Automation (ICRA), Shanghai, China, 9–13 May 2011

12. Shilane, P., Min, P., Kazhdan, M., Funkhouser, T.: The Princeton shape benchmark. In: Proceedings Shape Modeling Applications, pp. 167–178 (2004). https://doi.org/10.1109/SMI.2004.1314504

13. Welzl, E.: Smallest enclosing disks (balls and ellipsoids). In: Maurer, H. (ed.) New Results and New Trends in Computer Science. LNCS, vol. 555, pp. 359–370. Springer, Heidelberg (1991). https://doi.org/10.1007/BFb0038202

14. Yang, H.: Protein surface analysis by dimension reduction with applications in functional annotation and drug target prediction. Ph.D. thesis, Drexel University (2015)

E-Health

Proposal of a Smart Hospital Based on Internet of Things (IoT) Concept

Camilo Cáceres[1(✉)], João Mauricio Rosário[1], and Dario Amaya[2]

[1] University of Campinas (UNICAMP), Campinas, Brazil
{camilocf, rosario}@fem.unicamp.br
[2] Military University Nueva Granada (UMNG), Bogotá, Colombia
dario.amaya@unimilitar.edu.co

Abstract. This article proposes the utilization of the Artificial Intelligence (AI) and Automation techniques oriented to a service-based business. Developing and proposing a methodology for the implementation and development of a smart hospital, taking as a foundation a traditional hospital. The approach is based on the analysis of the studied e-health system, focusing on the patient flow. The use of Discrete Event Simulation (DES) models allows a computational model method for recreating the system and detect the system's bottlenecks. Those blockages are improved by the addition of "smart devices", implemented in the DES model and this improvement of the patient flow attendance and service quality, what directly influence the reduction of mortality in the Emergency Department (ED). Finally, the social implication is the reduction of the mortality in the ED, what is directly related to the improvement of the service quality and the reduction of the waiting time for the patients.

Keywords: E-health · Smart Hospital · Discrete Event Simulation

1 Introduction

Nowadays, due to the technological improvement, our life has been improved considerably, especially in cases like transportation, manufacturing, communications, businesses and other areas. The healthcare area has been improved also, but not as fast as other areas, due to the risks and special care it needs to improve.

The healthcare is highly represented by the medical services that are given in hospitals. Those hospitals offer a different kind of services and specializations, associated with the different patient requirements. In this work, the focus is the Emergency Department of a hospital, due to the critical management operation of the system and the critical need of the users.

The Emergency Department (ED) or Emergency Ward is an area of primary care, that aims to offer initial treatment of different diseases to patients with high priority who present themselves without a prior appointment. According to [1, 2] the EDs around the world show problems of overcrowding. In the study presented by [1], 15 developed countries were studied, and the high attendance produced overcrowding and a reduction of the service quality.

© Springer Nature Switzerland AG 2019
N. Lepore et al. (Eds.): SaMBa 2018, LNCS 11379, pp. 93–104, 2019.
https://doi.org/10.1007/978-3-030-13835-6_11

The overcrowding of patients in an ED is a situation that is presented when the number of patients is superior to the number of resources, whether medical staff, medical devices or hospital care areas. This situation leads to a considerable increase in patient waiting time and a reduction in efficiency and quality of service. The problem of overcrowding in ED is a generalized problem around the world [2, 3], a public health problem that affects everyone in every social class [1]. The key factors that generate the problem are mainly the duration of patients' waiting time, agglomerations, patients' inflow and outflow, physicians' productivity, available physical resources, among other factors [2, 3].

In recent years, different countries have adopted practices and action plans to reduce the effect of overcrowding, as those presented by [1, 2], but the adopted policies are not enough to solve the problem since variables such as uncertainty of patient flow, different types of diseases, and other external factors such as epidemics or natural disasters are difficult to predict.

The main implications of the overcrowding problem in ED are the decrease in quality of service, increased risk of death and social discrimination in the queues [4]. According to [4] the relation between the overcrowding in ED and the mortality rate have a high relation, and in 4 of 6 studies were found that the Late Treatment presents a relation with the mortality of the patients in the ED. Meanwhile, the other presented factors are not conclusive to indicate a considerable relation with the mortality rate in the emergency services.

From another viewpoint, for hospitals, the problem of overcrowding in the ED brings economic profits, since the service provided with overcrowding maximizes the use of resources and thus allows a better use of the available assets and personnel, thus maximizing the profit of the providers of health services [5]. Therefore, the proposals of solution for the overcrowding have as a minimum requirement: the improvement of the service quality and, at the same time, the improvement of the hospital's profit. These constraints make this problem a highly complex problem since it regards the quality of the provision of a high-risk service with the profit and maintenance of the hospital. It is important to highlight that overcrowding is not a daily problem and following one of the studies presented by [5], the problem occurs only in 25% of the total operating time of the ED, which increases the difficulty of the problem, due to the unpredictability of patient flow behavior.

Among the proposed solutions to solve the problem of overcrowding in the ED exists 2 kinds of solutions: the implementation of healthcare politics or the optimization of resources using management operation tools. Between the documented healthcare politics by American College of Emergency Physicians in 2008, the better policies are the reallocation of the admitted patients to free areas, such as corridors and conference rooms; coordination of surgeries scheduling, among other ideas, which, even offering improvements, they are not definitive solutions, presenting inconsistencies in the existing literature [4]. By another hand, the management operations view requires the use of simulation and optimization tools, which are used for an administrative view of healthcare management. The acceptance of the last approach in the healthcare field to test different and new methodologies, policies and operations are increasing; which is reflected in the increase of researches and publications in the area [6].

The different simulation paradigms can identify the complexity of healthcare systems, that are mainly three: Discrete Event Simulation (DES), System Dynamics (SD) and Agent-Based Modeling (ABM). The main difference between those system modeling paradigms is that in the first two (DES and SD) depend on rules defined in the real world, entities are modeled based on these rules. By another hand, the ABM, present an interaction between entities based on defined rules based on the behavior of the systems [7]. The biggest problems in healthcare systems can be optimized using simulation models, managing to improve problems such as high patient flow, patient scheduling, shift scheduling, testing of new health policies, among others [7].

By another hand, the use of the IoT and Industry 4.0 concepts in the healthcare is starting with high importance according to the potentially useful applications in the area [8]. To introduce some concepts, the Internet of Things (IoT), basically proposes a use, processing, and storage of information in the cloud, that can be accessed and used autonomously by intelligent objects with a connection in the cloud through the internet [9]. The goal of the IoT is the sharing of data and processing of them, to achieve a smart integration of the objects aimed at improving the life quality.

By the other side, the concept Industry 4.0 is based on the IoT principle of an intelligent connection of objects, in this case, information technologies (IT) and operational technologies (OT), to facilitate the development of each company's own services and processes. Industry 4.0 can also be called the Industrial Internet of Things (IIoT) following the vision proposed by the company General Electric [10].

In general, it is possible to realize that the IoT is a very extensive concept, the reason why the concept of Industry 4.0 presented as IIoT, is a study area that applies the concepts of the IoT in the industry, making both concepts complementary and highly related. In this work, the IoT and IIoT concepts are used as synonymous due to the similarity of the concept in the healthcare area.

The main idea of this work is to propose and present with a study case the convergence of the IoT concept and healthcare management. That convergence could be ambiguous, but in a wide view, the healthcare management using as input data the collected data by the IoT objects, related to the patients, can be extremely useful to know the state of the system and the possible improvements. Obtained information like queues lengths, waiting time and related data are extremely valuable for the implementation of a smart, connected and optimal solutions in hospital management, what will bring an improvement of quality in the different healthcare areas due to the better use of the resources.

The proposal of this study is to propose a potential solution to improve the main problem of the ED services, the overcrowding, due to its direct impact on the mortality rate in the ED. The methodology needs the use of the concept of IoT, a simulation tool as the DES, and other secondary concepts, like telemedicine and automatic control notions to achieve the goal.

2   Methodology

The following methodology is based on the data obtained from the ED model presented in [11], where the author developed a DES model of an ED and treated it as an optimization problem. In that project, the hospital data and information were summarized the into stochastic data, later reflected on the ED DES. After the collection of the dataset and the implementation of the DES model in Matlab 2017a® (SimEvents®), it is possible to reproduce the simulation and verify the improvement of the system.

Subsequent, the DES allows reading the different management data of the system. That information can be compared with some of the information obtained by the IoT system, following each patient in the ED, information like queue length in each station, the average waiting time of patients, and so on. That data is enough to observe the system as the IoT would look at it, with an administrative management perspective, allowing the implementation of an online control for the current system requirements.

Finally, the identification and improvement of the principal bottlenecks in the system. The simulation allows the detection of the main system bottlenecks and with that knowledge is possible to propose a feasible solution to solve that problem. The proposed solution is based on telemedicine and principles of automatic control, to control the flow of patients. Also, the additional investment in hospital personnel and the use of a service of telemedicine requires a little investment, compared with the hospital quality improvement.

2.1   Discrete Event Simulation (DES) for an Emergency Department (ED) Study Case

The implementation of the ED using DES is based on the data and simulation presented in [11], follows the stochastic data presented in Table 1 and Fig. 1.

Table 1. Service time distributions at each stage of the process.

Stage	Distribution (Minutes)
Reception	Uniform (5,10)
Lab tests	Triangular (10,20,30)
Examination room	Uniform (10,20)
Reexamination room	Uniform (7,12)
Sala De treatment room	Uniform (20,30)
Emergency room	Uniform (60,120)

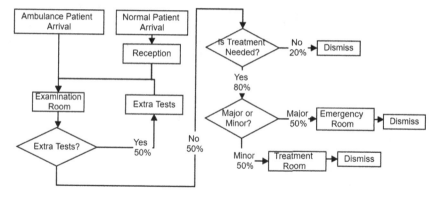

Fig. 1. Emergency department high-level process view, following the presented by [11]

As the Fig. 1 shows the inputs of patients correspond to a receptionist arrival and an ambulance arrival. The receptionist arrival corresponds to a non-homogenous Poisson process with an estimate of $\lambda(t)$ given in Fig. 2. Another hand gives the ambulance arrival process given by a Poisson process with a rate of 2 per hour.

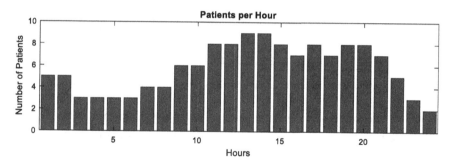

Fig. 2. Plot of the estimated rate function $\lambda(t)$ in patients per hour for the arrival process

The implementation of the simulation was made using Simulink® (SimEvents®) in Matlab 2017. The constants of the system that corresponds to the staff servers are presented in Table 2, as is presented in Fig. 3. The results obtained by the system, after 1000 simulations, can be observed in Table 3, where appears the main statistical information of the system behavior.

Table 2. Constant values for each staff server of the Fig. 3.

Staff server	Abbreviation	Current value
Reception	R	2
Doctor	D	2
Laboratory technician	T	3
TR nurse (Treatment room)	TN	1
ER nurse (Emergency room)	EN	9

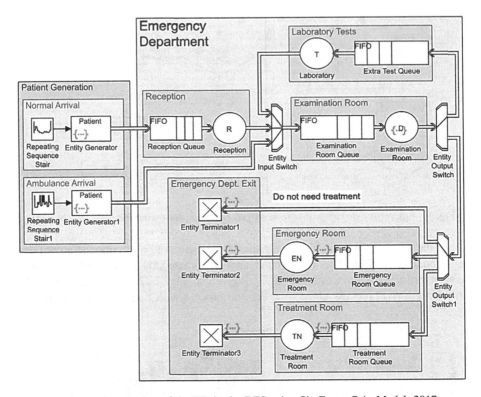

Fig. 3. Implementation of the ED in the DES using SimEvents® in Matlab 2017.

Table 3. Information about the main processes of the system presented in the Fig. 3.

Result	Value	Standard deviation
Expected patient time in system (h)	3.99	0.77
Expected number out (patients per hour)	4.85	0.35
Average waiting time (min): Reception	0.00	0.00
Average waiting time (min): Laboratory	0.70	0.50
Average waiting time (min): Doctor	**85.01**	**25.81**
Average waiting time (Min): Emergency room	0.03	0.34
Average waiting time (min): Treatment room	19.77	11.13
Average queue length: Reception	0.00	0.00
Average queue length: Laboratory	0.05	0.03
Average queue length: Doctor	**18.07**	**5.67**
Average queue length: Emergency room	0.00	0.01
Average queue length: Treatment room	1.00	0.54
Utilization (%): Reception	28.00	1.00
Utilization (%): Laboratory	5.00	5.00
Utilization (%): Doctor	**96.00**	**1.00**
Utilization (%): Emergency room	34.00	4.00
Utilization (%): Treatment room	64.00	9.00

2.2 Detection of the Bottlenecks and Proposed Solution

Based on the Table 3 can be observed that the utilization of the Examination Room is $96 \pm 1\%$, what is too high. Also, the queue length and the waiting time of patients there are so high, the queue length an average of 17.83 ± 5.55 patients and the waiting time an average of $84,67 \pm 25,62$ min, showing it as the main bottleneck in the system.

The proposed solution is based on the concept of telemedicine, specifically the use of Doctors using telepresence for the Examination Room. The concept of telemedicine has been applied in [12, 13], consequently currently with the implementation of concepts as IoT, that concept and use can be highly used with the inclusion of the new technologies in the society.

The proposal is an alternative Examination Room based on telepresence, what will allow that some doctors in a remote center be able to diagnose the patients. That idea will remove the detected bottleneck of the system.

2.3 Implementation of the Solution

The Smart Hospital concept is primarily based on the implementation of the telediagnosis room in the DES is introduced as a finite resource that depends on the queue length. The selected queue length is of 5 patients in the waiting line, the reason of that choice is that the current number of doctors in the physical room is 2 and the teledoctors is 2, so a waiting line of 5 leaves only 1 person waiting in line. The remote diagnosis center can maximumly assign 2 tele-doctors per turn, each turn is around 13,25 min, what is the average time a doctor diagnoses a patient.

For the control of the required number of doctors was used a concept of automatic control, the implementation of a PID (Proportional, Integral, and Derivative) controller what is highly used in robotics, industrial processes and others [14–16]. The implementation of that concept will allow a mathematical model to take some decisions according to the system error, the equation what model the implemented PID controller in the DES model is presented in the Eq. (1), where $u(t)$ is the control output signal, $e(t)$ the error signal, P the proportional control constant, I the integral control constant and D the derivative control constant.

$$u(t) = P\,e(t) + I \int e(t)dt + D\frac{de(t)}{dt} \tag{1}$$

To set the PID parameters of this system with stochastic and unknown dynamic model has been used an Artificial Intelligence technique, a Genetic Algorithm (GA) what is a metaheuristic optimization Evolutionary Algorithm. The GA optimizes by a metaheuristic the PID controller constants P, I and D, using a fitness function. A population of 100 PID constants represents the feasible solutions, that are evaluated by a fitness function where the more fit individuals of the population can survive, mutate, replicate, and reproduce themselves to obtain better results. Examples of optimization of different controllers in different applications and with different controllers or neuro-controllers using GAs can be found in [17–19].

The used GA follows the proposal made by [17], where the fitness function corresponds to the algebraic sum of 3 methods to evaluate PID controllers, the Integral

Square Error (ISE), Integral Absolute Error (IAE) and Integral of Time-Weighted Absolute Error (ITAE) methods is cost or fitness function (*J*) that the GA should optimize. The fitness function (*J*) follows the Eq. (2).

$$J(P, I, D) = \int_0^\infty [e(t)]^2 dt + \int_0^\infty |e(t)| dt + \int_0^\infty t|e(t)| dt \qquad (2)$$

The genetic algorithm implemented in this proposal follows the procedure shown in Fig. 4.

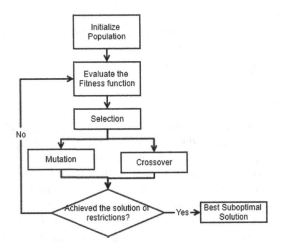

Fig. 4. Flow diagram of the genetic algorithm.

By another hand, the implemented PID controller has a limited and rounded output. The rounded output is given because the number of doctors is an integer positive number. The minimum number obtained can be 0 and the maximum is 2, it is a constraint for the number of tele-doctors.

3   Results and Discussion

The implementation of the Smart Hospital ED is based in the traditional hospital ED, just adding a PID controller to requiring the telepresence doctor service. After the implementation of the telediagnosis center, it was possible to identify the creation of a new bottleneck in the Treatment Room (TR), so a treatment nurse was added to improve this new issue.

The implementation of the PID controller to control the number of required doctors allowed to improve the results given by [11], that was also presented in Table 3. The PID controller was adjusted with the following constants: *P = 0.3012, I = 0.00984* and *D = 0.000498*. The results after 1000 simulations with the proposed controller are presented in Table 4.

Table 5 presents the differences between the traditional hospital and the Smart Hospital proposal, the values in bold located in the *Difference* column show the improved data.

Table 4. Information on the key performances of the Smart Hospital (1000 simulations).

Result	Value	Standard deviation
Expected time in system (h): Total	2.54	0.33
Expected number out (patients per hour): Total	6.20	0.47
Average waiting time (min): Reception	0.00	0.00
Average waiting time (min): Laboratory	6.15	4.59
Average waiting time (min): Doctor	**23.13**	**1.80**
Average waiting time (min): Emergency room	0.44	1.10
Average waiting time (min): Treatment room	3.87	2.30
Average queue length: Reception	0.00	0.00
Average queue length: Laboratory	0.69	0.62
Average queue length: Doctor	**5.45**	**0.75**
Average queue length: Emergency room	0.02	0.07
Average queue length: Treatment room	0.25	0.12
Utilization (%): Reception	29.00	1.00
Utilization (%): Laboratory	58.00	8.00
Utilization (%): Doctor	94.00	2.00
Utilization (%): Emergency room	39.00	6.00
Utilization (%): Treatment room	39.00	5.00

Table 5. Comparison of the key performances of a traditional and the Smart Hospital proposal.

Result	Hospital value	Smart Hospital value	Difference
Expected time in system (h)	3.73	2.84	**0.89**
Expected number out (patients per hour)	4.72	6.38	**−1.66**
Average waiting time (min): Reception	0.00	0.00	0.00
Average waiting time (min): Laboratory	0.59	6.05	−5.47
Average waiting time (min): Doctor	85.02	23.15	**61.87**
Average waiting time (min): Emergency room	0.03	0.44	−0.41
Average waiting time (min): Treatment room	19.91	3.89	**16.02**
Average queue length: Reception	0.00	0.00	0.00
Average queue length: Laboratory	0.05	0.69	−0.64
Average queue length: Doctor	18.22	5.39	**12.83**
Average queue length: Emergency room	0.00	0.02	−0.02
Average queue length: Treatment room	0.77	0.30	**0.47**
Utilization (%): Reception	28.00	29.00	–
Utilization (%): Laboratory	5.00	58.00	–
Utilization (%): Doctor	96.00	94.00	–
Utilization (%): Emergency room	34.00	39.00	–
Utilization (%): Treatment room	64.00	39.00	–

Based on Table 5 is possible to see the improvements of the hospital in different ways, between the most remarkable results, are the reduction of the user time in the system by 0.89 h, the increased number of output patients by 1.66 patients more per hour, the reduction by 61.87 min of the average waiting time for the doctors are the most remarkable changes in the system.

By another hand, some results were negatively affected, but the decreased behavior is not significant to affect the system or to reduce the quality of the obtained results. Therefore, the patients will see a significant improvement in the ED, reducing the mortality rate according to [4].

The comparison between the used resources by each case is presented in Table 6, where is possible to see the modifications between the systems and understand the additional required staff to improve the ED quality according to the Table 5.

Table 6. Comparison of the Staff Number in 24 h of service.

Staff server	Abbreviation	Hospital	Smart Hospital
Reception	R	2	2
Doctor	D	2	2
Telepresence doctor (Dynamically controlled)	–	–	**0.6683 ± 0.1672**
Laboratory technician	T	3	3
TR nurse (Treatment room)	TN	1	**2**
ER nurse (Emergency room)	EN	9	9

By observing the Table 6 is possible to infer that the Smart Hospital system added 1 Nurse of TR and the equivalent of a 0.6683 ± 0.1672 tele-doctors (in a day). That increase in the staff number has improved the ED system as is presented in Tables 4 and 5. Those improvements affect directly the system performance by reduction of the user time in the system by 1.18 h and the increased number output patients by 1.66 patients more per hour, what are significant changes from the patients' viewpoint, helping to save lives in risk and allowing a higher quality service in the ED services.

4 Conclusion and Further Developments

The IoT and IIoT concepts can be used in different areas for different purposes, for example in the performance improvement of any service-based system. In this case, a healthcare system was presented, and by the example of an ED was shown the implementation possibilities and uses of connected things to obtain data and improve the administration and management of a queue-based system with the help of current technological solutions.

The perspective of the IoT and IIoT used in a simulation, as it was presented in this work using DES, allowing the possibility to prototype real solutions without the implementation of real smart objects, making feasible a simulated environment to test smart policies based IoT captured data.

The inclusion of robotics and other current technologies in smart environments, using this simulation approach is feasible when the system can be approached as a stochastic system. The multi-agent-based simulation will be an opportunity to simulate and test in depth the concept of connected smart devices in a more realistic and controlled environment.

By another hand, the improvement of the ED, in the smart hospital case was successful, using not many additional resources and a concept as telemedicine and IoT, the system improved by around 30% in the expected number of output patients and patient expected time in the system. Those significant changes were obtained by an addition of 10% of the old staff, according to the presented results.

Finally, it was possible to present a work were the IoT, IIoT, the DES, and other current technological concepts converged in the result of an improved environment, what leads to a futuristic and not so distant world, where the smart connected devices will allow an improvement of the resources uses improving the life quality of the society.

References

1. Pines, J.M., et al.: International perspectives on emergency department crowding. Acad. Emerg. Med. **18**(12), 1358–1370 (2011)
2. Bittencourt, R.J., Hortale, V.A.: Intervenções para solucionar a superlotação nos serviços de emergência hospitalar: uma revisão sistemática. Cad. Saúde Publica **25**(7), 1439–1454 (2009)
3. Jensen, K.: Emergency department crowding: the nature of the problem and why it matters. In: Hall, R. (ed.) Patient flow: reducing delay in healthcare delivery, vol. 206, pp. 97–105. Springer, New York (2013). https://doi.org/10.1007/978-1-4614-9512-3_4
4. McHugh, M.: The consequences of emergency department crowding and delays for patients. In: Hall, R. (ed.) Patient flow: reducing delay in healthcare delivery, pp. 107–127. Springer, New York (2013). https://doi.org/10.1007/978-1-4614-9512-3_5
5. Handel, D.A., Hilton, J.A., Ward, M.J., Rabin, E., Zwemer, F.L., Pines, J.M.: Emergency department throughput, crowding, and financial outcomes for hospitals. Acad. Emerg. Med. **17**(8), 840–847 (2010)
6. Thorwarth, M., Arisha, A.: Application of discrete-event simulation in health care: a review, Dublin (2009)
7. Oueida, S., Char, P.A., Kadry, S., Ionescu, S.: Simulation models for enhancing the health care systems. FAIMA Bus. Manag. J. **4**(4), 5–20 (2016)
8. Islam, S.M.R., Kwak, D., Kabir, M.H., Hossain, M., Kwak, K.-S.: The Internet of Things for health care: a comprehensive survey. IEEE Access **3**, 678–708 (2015)
9. Bradley, D., Russell, D., Ferguson, I., Isaacs, J., MacLeod, A., White, R.: The Internet of Things – the future or the end of mechatronics. Mechatronics **27**, 57–74 (2015)
10. Gilchrist, A.: Industry 4.0. Apress, Berkeley (2016)
11. Ahmed, M.A., Alkhamis, T.M.: Simulation optimization for an emergency department healthcare unit in Kuwait. Eur. J. Oper. Res. **198**(3), 936–942 (2009)
12. Latifi, R., et al.: Telemedicine and telepresence for trauma and emergency care management. Scand. J. Surg. **96**(4), 281–289 (2007)
13. Marconi, G.P., Chang, T., Pham, P.K., Grajower, D.N., Nager, A.L.: Traditional nurse triage vs physician telepresence in a pediatric ED. Am. J. Emerg. Med. **32**(4), 325–329 (2014)

14. Beleño, R.D.H., et al.: Dynamic modeling and PID control of an underwater robot based on the hardware-in-the-loop method. Int. Rev. Mech. Eng. **10**(7), 482 (2016)
15. Chou, C.-Y., Juang, C.-F.: Navigation of an autonomous wheeled robot in unknown environments based on evolutionary fuzzy control. Inventions **3**(1), 3 (2018)
16. Siciliano, B., Khatib, O.: Springer Handbook of Robotics, 2nd edn. Springer, Cham (2016). https://doi.org/10.1007/978-3-319-32552-1
17. Jayachitra, A., Vinodha, R.: Genetic algorithm based PID controller tuning approach for continuous stirred tank reactor. Adv. Artif. Intell. **2014**, 1–8 (2014)
18. Cáceres Flórez, C.A., Rosário, J.M., Amaya, D.: Control structure for a car-like robot using artificial neural networks and genetic algorithms. Neural Comput. Appl., 1–14 (2018). https://doi.org/10.1007/s00521-018-3514-1
19. Caceres, C., Rosario, J.M., Amaya, D.: Approach of kinematic control for a nonholonomic wheeled robot using artificial neural networks and genetic algorithms. In: International Conference and Workshop on Bioinspired Intelligence (IWOBI), pp. 1–6 (2017)

A Web-Based Telepathology Framework for Collaborative Work of Pathologists to Support Teaching and Research in Latin America

Darwin Díaz[1], Germán Corredor[2], Eduardo Romero[2], and Angel Cruz-Roa[1(✉)]

[1] GITECX Research Group, AdaLab Research Seedbed, Universidad de los Llanos, Villavicencio, Colombia
{darwin.diaz,aacruz}@unillanos.edu.co
[2] CIM@LAB Research Group, Universidad Nacional de Colombia, Bogotá, Colombia
{gcorredor,edromero}@unal.edu.co

Abstract. Early diagnosis in cancer is very important for an appropriate treatment and effective recovery in some cases. The biggest problem in developing countries, such as Latin America, is the delay of diagnosis because poor availability of health services in remote regions and lack of pathologists who are concentrated in main cities. In this context, this paper presents a web-based telepathology framework for collaborative work of pathologists. The evaluation was addressed to analyze the computational performance in terms of time response when several and concurrent simulated user's navigations of whole-slide images are performed. The preliminary results show that the framework is able to support concurrent users with an average response time of 10 s when navigations is performed at the same magnification, which increases until 35 s in average when navigation includes changes of magnification.

Keywords: Digital pathology · Telepathology · Whole-slide imaging

1 Introduction

For diseases such as cancer, early diagnosis is a very important factor to guarantee an appropriate treatment and an effective recovery in tractable cases. An important problem in developing countries (e.g., Latin America) is the lack of access to health services and specialized personnel in medical centers with the capacity to handle the different phases of pathology: digitization of slides, diagnosis assisted by pathologists, prognosis, and treatment [6].

Technology advances have been successfully incorporated in health care in the last decades. In the pathology context, tissue sample scanners from different providers have enabled the digitalization of histopathology samples into whole-slide images (WSIs), thereby boosting the area of digital pathology and cancer research [5]. Unfortunately, slide scanners are still very expensive, around

© Springer Nature Switzerland AG 2019
N. Lepore et al. (Eds.): SaMBa 2018, LNCS 11379, pp. 105–112, 2019.
https://doi.org/10.1007/978-3-030-13835-6_12

$175.000 USD, which has limited its wide use in developing countries. For this reason, some innovative alternatives have emerged such as the design and development of low-cost motorized microscope for telepathology and digitalization of pathology slides [2,7,9]. However, despite the potential benefits such technologies might offer to remote regions by means of telepathology practices, there are very few efforts to include analysis of digital pathological samples in health systems around Latin America.

The rest of paper is organized as follows: Sect. 2 describes definitions and previous works in digital pathology and telepathology. Section 3 presents the web-based telepathology framework for pathologists collaborative work. Section 4 describes the experimental setup to evaluate the framework in terms of time response versus number of concurrent users. Section 5 presents the experimental results. Finally, Sect. 6 presents some conclusions and future directions.

2 Previous Works

2.1 Digital Pathology

Digital pathology is an emerging research area defined as the set of computational and technological methods that support the different stages of the pathology workflow (See Fig. 1), including slide digitization, computer-aided diagnosis, prognosis, and treatment [8].

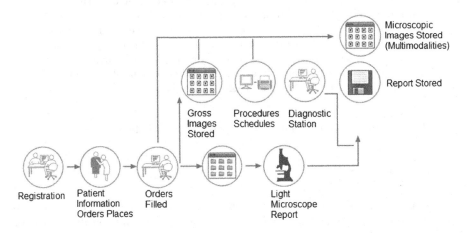

Fig. 1. Traditional pathology vs digital pathology workflow. Adapted from: [4]

2.2 Telemedicine and Telepathology

Telemedicine is defined as the provision of remote health services in the components of promotion, prevention, diagnosis, treatment and rehabilitation, by professional personnel using Information and Communication Technologies (ICT), which facilitates the access to information and offers the opportunity to reach isolated populations [1].

Technological advances for digitalization of whole slides of histopathology (using robotic microscopies and slide scanners) have opened different innovative services such as diagnosis of slides at distance, telepathology, large-scale histopathology image data bases, computer-assisted diagnosis, among others [3].

Telepathology is one of those innovative services. It is defined as the practice of remote pathology by means of the transmission of macroscopic and/or microscopic digital images through communication networks to provide diagnostic services, collaborative research, teaching, and consultations remotely. Telepathology has two main different implementations. Fist, a histopathology slide into a robotic microscope is controlled by specialized personnel remotely by the transmission of the field of view of the slide, which is visualized through a computer monitor in other location; this approach, however, demands proper connection resources. Second, the histopathology slides are fully digitized in the remote areas (where the patient is located), and then they are analyzed in a web application by pathologists at distance.

The second implementation of telepathology is particularly interesting for the Latin American context since it enables access to pathology services in remote areas where is difficult to have pathologists and the bandwidth is limited. In the next section, a web-based telepathology framework is presented; it allows users to simultaneously access, navigate, annotate, and analyze digitalized whole-slide histopathology images.

3 Web-Based Telepathology Framework

Figure 2 depicts our proposed implementation of a Web-based telepathology framework for collaborative work of pathologists. First, our solution is a Web application with a user interface (UI) based on Bootstrap[1] and Java Server Pages (JSP)[2] that provides, by authentication, access to multiple users (pathologists) using a standard web browser. The Web application comprises two main modules: (i) a whole-slide histopathology image viewer (`SlideViewer`), and (ii) a whole-slide histopathology image data resource provider (`WSIProvider`).

Whole-Slide Histopathology Image Viewer. The `SlideViewer` module is an interface between the user (who uses a web-based user interface) and the `WSIProvider` module. It displays the image regions requested by the user through the web browser. When a pathologist interacts with the user interface (panning or zooming), the corresponding image regions are requested to `WSIProvider` and then displayed.

---

[1] https://getbootstrap.com/.

[2] https://docs.oracle.com/javaee/6/tutorial/doc/bnaay.html.

Whole-Slide Histopathology Image Data Resource Provider. The WSIProvider is an interface between the SlideViewer module and the data resources stored in a data server. Such resources include the images (stored in different formats such as SVS, JPEG2000, or TIFF), data indexes, thumbnails, diagnostic information, and annotations. This module uses the Jasper 2.0[3] implementation for decodification of JPEG2000 images and OpenSlide[4] for other image formats.

In order to analyze the viability of this Web-based telepathology framework, an experimental setup is defined to evaluate the response times when different simulated simultaneous users navigate the whole-slide histopathology images.

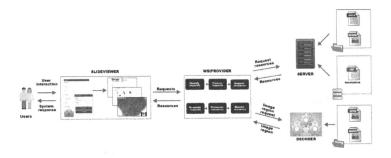

Fig. 2. Overall scheme of the proposed implementation of a Web-based telepathology framework for collaborative work of pathologists.

4   Experimental Setup

The evaluation of the web-based telepathology framework was performed in terms of response times of tile requests from the UI during the whole-slide histopathology image navigation. Four different predefined navigations were designed to evaluate the response times when whole-slide histopathology images are navigated in a concurrent manner for one or more users (1, 2, 4, 8). Each combination of a given navigation and concurrent user was repeated 10 times to calculate the average and dispersion of response times in order to analyze the stability and robustness of the web-based telepathology framework in a typical scenario with limited bandwidth and several pathologists or pathology residents exploring and analyzing different whole-slide histopathology images at the same time. All the experiments were executed in server with Debian 8 OS, 32 GB RAM, a CPU processor with 32 logic cores, and maximum memory for JVM was fixed into 20 GB.

---

[3] https://www.ece.uvic.ca/~frodo/jasper/.

[4] https://openslide.org/.

4.1   Performace Measure

The response time of the tile's requests of regions from the whole-slide histopathology image according to UI field-view of the web-based telepathology framework was the real time of execution of the slide navigation, or Elapsed time (E_t). The elapsed time was calculated as the difference between the initial time measurement when the navigation starts with the first set of tiles required for the initial visualization of WSI t_i and the final time when the navigation ends with the last tile required shown in the screen t_f, such as it is presented in Eq. (1).

$$E_t = t_f - t_i \tag{1}$$

4.2   Simulated Navigations

In order to evaluate in an objective manner the computational performance of the web-based telepathology framework, four different navigations were defined. According to the UI of the web-based telepathology framework, there are a fixed set of actions to explore the whole-slide histopathology images by users: (i) loading of the image, (ii) the displacement (vertical or horizontal), and, (iii) zoom-in and zoom-out in different magnifications between 0.1× and 40×. Hence, four simulated navigations were defined starting from above actions as follows:

Navigation 1. The first navigation consisted of the loading of the image at 4× magnification, as it is shown in Fig. 3.

Fig. 3. Navigation 1: Load of tiles from the whole-slide image at 4× magnification.

Navigation 2. The second navigation consisted of: (i) loading the image in 4× magnification, (ii) magnification transition 4× to 10×, and, (iii) magnification transition 10× to 40×, as it is shown in Fig. 4.

Navigation 3. The third navigation consisted of: (i) the loading of the image in magnification 4×, and (ii) displacement of the central zone towards the upper right area of the image, as it is shown in Fig. 5.

Fig. 4. Navigation 2: Load of tiles from the whole-slide image at 4× magnification, zoom-in from 4× to 10×, zoom-in from 10× to 40×.

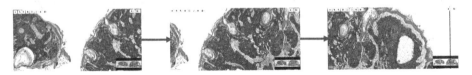

Fig. 5. Navigation 3: Load of tiles from the whole-slide image at 4× magnification and displacement of the central zone towards the upper right area of the image.

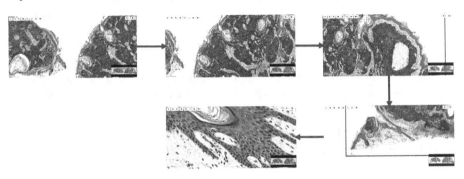

Fig. 6. Navigation 4: Load of tiles from the whole-slide image at 4× magnification, displacement of the central zone towards the upper right area of the image, jump to lower left area, and, zoom-in from 4× to 40×.

Navigation 4. The fourth navigation consisted of: (i) loading the image in 4× magnification, (ii) moving the central area towards the upper right area of the image, (iii) jumping to the lower left area, and, (iv) magnification 4× to 40×, As shown in Fig. 6.

5   Results

Figure 7 presents the experimental results for each of four navigations by comparing the number of concurrent users performing each navigation versus response time in seconds. Figure 7A shows that Navigation 1 took around of 7.5 s for 1, 2 and 4 concurrent users and close to 8.5 s in average for 8 concurrent users. Figure 7B shows increasing time for Navigation 2 with an average of 30 s for 1 concurrent user, 30.5 in average for 2 users, 33.5 in average for 4 concurrent users and 40.5 s for 8 concurrent users. Figure 7C depicts that Navigation 3 took 11.5 s

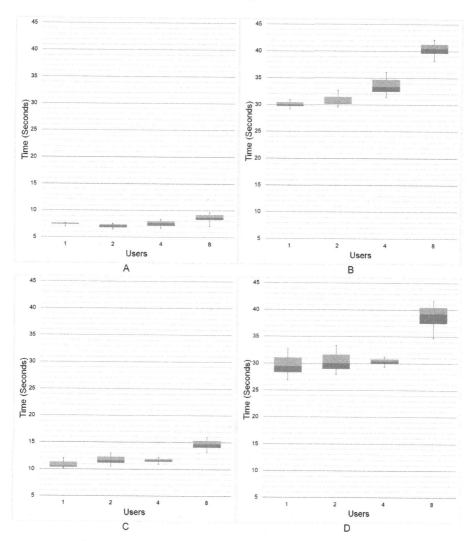

Fig. 7. Boxplots of the execution times in seconds of each navigation with a particular number of concurrent users (1, 2, 4 and 8). (A) Navigation 1, (B) Navigation 2, (C) Navigation 3, and D Navigation 4.

in average fro 1, 2 and 4 concurrent users and 14.5 in average for 8 concurrent users. Figure 7D shows that Navigation 4 took in average 30 s for 1, 2 and 4 concurrent users, whereas for 8 concurrent users took in average 39.5 s.

Therefore, Fig. 7A and C shows that the faster navigations results correspond to Navigation 1 and Navigation 3. Navigation 1 is just the load of an image at 4× magnification and Navigation 3 is the load of an image at 4× magnification and displacement from the central region towards the upper right area of the image at the same magnification. In contrast, Fig. 7B and D took more time because both Navigation 2 and Navigation 4 included changes of magnification. For instance, Navigation 2 changed the magnification from 4× to 10× and then from 10× to 40×, whereas Navigation 4 starts loading the image followed by vertical and horizontal displacements, then a jump to other unseen region and changed the magnification from 4× to 40×.

6   Conclusions and Future Directions

This paper presented a Web-based telepathology framework for pathologists collaborative work. For that, the implementations integrates different technologies and an evaluation was performed in order to analyze the capabilities for concurrent navigations from different users into whole-slide histopathology images. These results suggest that depending of the type request the response time changes. Here, displacements took less time in comparison to jumps and magnification changes. In addition, the response time increases as soon as the number of concurrent navigations are performed on the server.

Future work includes an evaluation of the framework with real pathologists from different locations, with more users working in concurrent manner over same whole-slide histopathology images and performance optimization of the queue tile's requests, by comparing multiple servers, distributed computing or GPU optimization.

References

1. Colombian Congress. Law 1419 of December 13 of 2010 (2010)
2. Cruz, A.: Data-Driven Representation Learning from Histopathology Image Databases to Support Digital Pathology Analysis, 1:164 (2015)
3. Farahani, N., Pantanowitz, L.: Overview of Telepathology (2015)
4. González López, A.M.: Las TIC como factor de Cambio. Technical report, Sescam, Satec (2011)
5. Gurcan, M.N., Boucheron, L.E., Can, A., Madabhushi, A., Rajpoot, N.M., Yener, B.: Histopathological image analysis: a review (2009)
6. Huang, C.H., Veillard, A., Roux, L., Loménie, N., Racoceanu, D.: Time-efficient sparse analysis of histopathological whole slide images. Comput. Med. Imaging Graph. **35**(7–8), 579–591 (2011)
7. Lasso, C., Vargas, C., Romero, E.: Sistema modular de telepatologia para la exploración remota de placas histopatoloogicas sobre la red renata. e-colabora (2012)
8. Madabhushi, A.: Digital pathology image analysis: opportunities and challenges. Imaging Med. **1**(1), 7–10 (2009)
9. Vargas, C., Romero, E.: Dispositivo para controlar la platina de un microscopio con la ayuda de un computador (2008)

Motor Analysis and Biosignals

Proposal of Methodology of a Bipedal Humanoid Gait Generation Based on Cognitive Algorithm

João Maurício Rosário$^{(\boxtimes)}$, Renato Suekichi Kuteken,
and Luis Miguel Izquierdo Cordoba

Faculdade de Engenharia Mecânica, Universidade Estadual de Campinas,
Campinas, SP, Brazil
rosario@fem.unicamp.br

Abstract. This article proposes a methodology of generating a bipedal humanoid gait pattern for the knee and hip leg joints in the sagittal plane. The multi-
functional gait movement is divided into three different movement patterns with
a specific function, which can be modulated individually and superposed to
compose a gait pattern. This strategy is based on the potential field navigation
algorithm concept (proposed by Khatib, 1986) and the architecture for its
application is based the AuRA cognitive architecture (proposed by Arkin, 1990).
Finally, this methodology was validated using a MATLAB-Simulink^{TM}
implementation of a simplified kinematic model of the legs movements. The
results show movement patterns close to the biomechanical ones at the joints.
When applied to the kinematic model, those joint movements generate feet
trajectories that are compatible to the gait both in shape and amplitude. The
strategy was also embedded in a microcontroller prototype, revealing low
computational demands as well as another view for the generated movement.

1 Introduction

The human gait is an activity that requires coordination of the nervous and the mus-
culoskeletal system [9] and can be described as a succession of "controlled falls" with
the intention of moving the body forward [8]. The gait presents 2 phases: the swing
phase and the stance phase, which can be single stance or double stance. During the
stance phase the muscles which are responsible for the dynamic balance are activated,
whereas during swing phase the lower limb is flexed and moves forward to hit the
ground in front of the individual. The gait mechanism can be represented by two
alternating models in the sagittal plane: the double pendulum (swing phase) and the
inverted pendulum (single stance phase) [6].

The gait is a task that adapts to different terrain conditions by changing the
movement patterns of the 3 lower limb joints (hip, knee and ankle). The adaptation for
the uphill gait usually requires increasing flexion angles on the three lower limb joints,
the greater the slope of the ground. During downhill gait, the hip joints present
decreasing flexion angles (between the half of the swing phase and the beginning of the

© Springer Nature Switzerland AG 2019
N. Lepore et al. (Eds.): SaMBa 2018, LNCS 11379, pp. 115–126, 2019.
https://doi.org/10.1007/978-3-030-13835-6_13

stance phase) while the knee joints present increasing flexion angles (in the beginning and in the end of the stance phase), the greater the slope of the ground [2].

Despite the evident complexity, after a person's cognitive learning period of time, the gait movement is performed almost automatically, without great coordination efforts or the need of conscious reasoning for its planning and execution [6]. While the human gait emerges from a combination of neural and mechanical systems, making the transference of those strategies to a robotic platform is not a trivial work [3].

Since the gait is a time dependent task, it requires a rapid response to environment changes, making unfeasible the use of extensive libraries of motion capture data to recreate the gait artificially. Thus, it becomes interesting to present this knowledge in the form of general rules that permit the movement generation in real time. One possible way to achieve this would be by applying artificial intelligence concepts, aiming at the replication some of the cognitive mechanisms involved with the gait.

This paper proposes an artificial gait generation in the sagittal plane by means of the superposition of three reference signals to the leg. It's subdivided in five parts. The part II, Kinematic Model, describes a brief description of the human body's relevant biomechanics aspects and kinematic model. The part III, Gait Generation Strategy, presents the cognitive architectures that served as a base for this work, as well the proposed architecture. The part IV, Validation Method, will be briefly explained, the methodology used for validation of proposal architecture. The part V, Experimental Implementation, will be presented the experimental platform, the computational simulations and their results, and, finally, the part VI will present the discussion and conclusions of this work.

2 Kinematic Model

2.1 Human Body

Before talking about a biped humanoid robotic platform and how to apply typical human body's movement strategies, it is necessary to understand the human body itself and how it is presented and described in the literature. The Fig. 1 shows the Biological Physical System with motion capture (mocap) markers (a); the physical system illustration [7] showing the 3 planes used to describe the body's movements (b); the simplified representation of the lower limbs (c), with the links lengths calculated as a proportion of the body height (H) with ratios value obtained from Rodacki, 2013 [10]; and the simplified representation of one leg in the sagittal plane, with θ and ζ as the angles on the hip and knee joins respectively (d).

The Fig. 2 shows the reference input for the desired artificially replicated movements is usually obtained from motion captures done with markers correspond the hip and knee movement angles related to the normal gait in the sagittal plane [10].

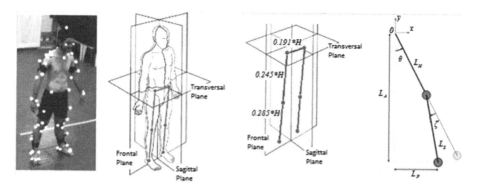

Fig. 1. Biological system and simplified representation of the lower limbs and of one leg in the sagittal plane.

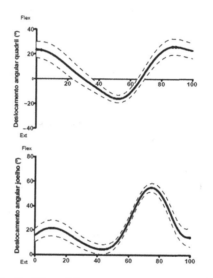

Fig. 2. Hip and knee movement angles. [10].

2.2 Kinematic Model

The biological physical system in the sagittal plane (Fig. 1) was used for the kinematic modeling of the legs, with the estimate lengths of the legs links (L_h and L_s) being calculated as a proportion of the body height (H). Thus, the position of the foot (end-effector) in the sagittal plane is described by the legs kinematics, with the joint angles (θ and ζ) (Table 1).

$$L_p = \sin(\theta)L_H + \sin(\theta - \zeta)L_s \tag{1}$$

$$L_A = \cos(\theta)L_H + \cos(\theta - \zeta)L_s \tag{2}$$

Table 1. Bodyparameters used in the kinematic model.

Symbol	Parameter
H	Body height
L_P	Horizontal linear position
L_A	Vertical linear position
L_H	Femur length (generally at 0.285*H)
L_S	Tibia length (generally at 0.285*H)
θ	Angle between Femur and vertical axis (y)
ζ	Angle between Tibia and Femur

3   Gait Generation Strategy

The architecture proposed in this work was inspired by the command superposition concept, present in the potential fields navigation proposed by Khatib [5] and in the Autonomous Robot Architecture (AuRA), proposed by Arkin [11].

Khatib proposed the superposition of attraction and repulsion fields, linked to goals and obstacles on a map. This allows for the emergence of a low level control, reactive to the map position and capable of guiding an embodied cognitive agent towards its goal while avoiding collisions.

AuRA on the other hand, develops a hybrid deliberative/reactive approach to robotic navigation. In this approach, control takes place initially in a hierarchic upper layer where the embodied cognitive agent's actions are planned, then proceeding to a reactive layer where sensing and actuation cycles are executed.

These reactive approaches are especially interesting when considering the neural structures known as Central Pattern Generators (CPG). Those structures work as a low-level control for the human body, being capable of generating locomotion patterns even when isolated from the supra-spinal nervous system [1], indicating that the gait is a reactive behavior, more than just deliberative.

In a similar way to the AuRA, the proposed architecture suggests an algorithm divided in 2 layers: hierarchical and reactive layer (Fig. 3).

3.1   Hierarchical Layer

There are 3 parts in the hierarchical layer:

- **The internal model of the world:** consists of the terrain information and the kinematic and dynamic models of the body, with the current status of the physical system. It is correspondent to the embodied cognitive agent's external environment awareness and body awareness (proprioception);
- **The mission planner:** consists of a higher-level decision block, responsible for choosing which task will be executed. Here, this part is just an interface for internal model viewing and a data input for user commands;
- **Plan selector:** consists of a list of predetermined parameter configurations meant to compose tasks using the behavior blocks in the reactive layer. Depending on the task chosen by the mission planner, a different configuration is selected by the plan selector.

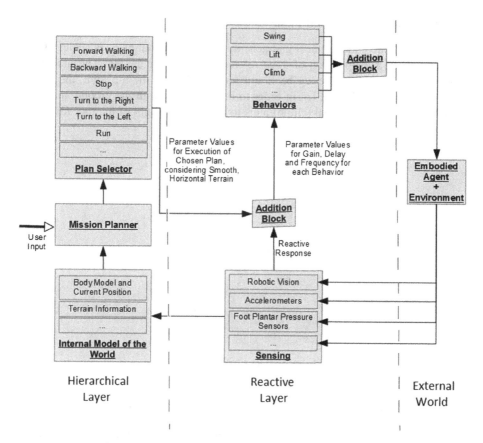

Fig. 3. Proposed cognitive architecture for gait generation.

3.2 Reactive Layer

The reactive layer has 2 parts:

- **The sensing part:** consists of the receipt of physical measurements by the embodied agent's sensors. These data are then used to feed the internal world model in the hierarchical layer and to formulate small adjustments that will be added to the configuration parameters defined by the hierarchical layer's plan selector part.
- **The behaviors part:** are a set of simple command signals, being executed in parallel and summed up to compose the reference signal that will be sent to the embodied agent's actuators. These command signals are modulated by the configuration parameters defined by the hierarchical layer's plan selector part and adjusted by the reactive layer's sensing part.

3.3   The Gait in the Sagittal Plane

As previously stated, the artificial gait generation in the sagittal plane is achieved here by means of the superposition of three reference signals for the leg. The first signal (swing) aims to oscillate the leg back and forth by flexing the hip joint, the second signal (lift) aims to raise the leg in order to break contact with the ground and avoid obstacles, and the third signal (climb) aims to correct the height of the foot for proper reestablishment of contact with the ground (Fig. 4).

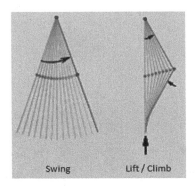

Fig. 4. Swing and Lift/Climb behaviors.

As previously stated, the artificial gait generation in the sagittal plane is achieved here by means of the superposition of three reference signals for the leg. The first signal (Swing) aims to oscillate the leg back and forth by flexing the hip joint, the second signal (lift) aims to raise the leg in order to break contact with the ground and avoid obstacles, and the third signal (climb) aims to correct the height of the foot for proper reestablishment of contact with the ground (Fig. 4).

4   Validation Method

The proposed algorithm will be validated by a MATLAB^{TM} simulation and an experimental implementation (Fig. 5).

The simulation will begin with a test of the behavior superposition principle, considering a horizontal level terrain, and the resulting signal will be compared to the biomechanical gait reference values from the literature for the hip and knee joints. After, the generated angles will be tested with the kinematic model of the legs in the sagittal plane and the feet trajectory will be observed both in the inertial reference system and in the non-inertial reference system, relative to the hip, and finally, the gait generation algorithm will be adapted and embedded in the experimental setup.

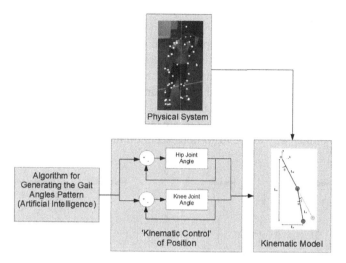

Fig. 5. Architecture validation.

5 Experimental Implementation and Results

The proposed gait generation algorithm was adapted and embedded in an experimental implementation platform with analogous proportions to the human body's average. The mechanism links were built from aluminum profile, the actuation on its degrees of freedom is performed by servo motors and the overall system control is carried by a microcontroller (Fig. 6).

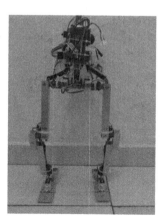

Fig. 6. Experimental implementation platform

The experimental implementation platform allowed for checking the possibility of embedding the algorithm and also allowed for visualizing the gait movement's execution. Those results can be accessed through the web address: https://www.youtube.com/embed/Q_b–LMoKgE?controls=0&start=6.

5.1   Simulation Results

Figure 7 shows the results of the superposition of the swing, Lift and Climb signals, with parameters fitted to replicate a gait pattern on level terrain. As an overall, the simulation results indicate the emergence of an artificial gait pattern close to the biomechanical gait pattern both in shape and amplitude when compared to the reference literature pattern showed on Fig. 2.

When the lift and climb behavior gains are increased, the superposed result becomes distorted in a similar way to the distortions seem on the biomechanical uphill gait.

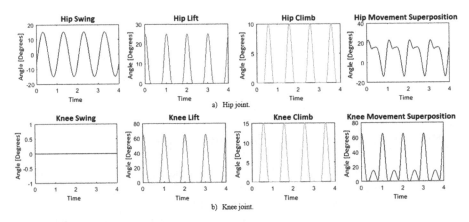

Fig. 7. Swing, Lift and Climb behavior signals for the Hip and knee joints and the signal composed by their superposition.

Figure 8 shows the graphs containing the results for the hip and knee joints relative to arbitrary changes in these gains. Literature graphs containing the angular values for

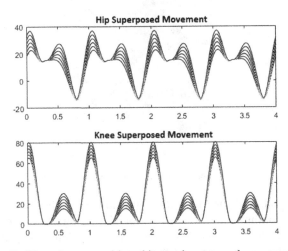

Fig. 8. Distortions caused by arbitrary changes on the parameters.

the joints as a function of the terrain slope steepness [2] are also presented, in Fig. 9, as a reference and for comparison purposes.

The graphs from Fig. 8 show an increased amplitude of the gait pattern around the region in between heel contact and weight acceptance point and around the toe off point, which means that this modified pattern presents a higher heel contact and a greater foot lift. Those distortions caused by arbitrary changes on the parameters of the Lift and Climb signals, supposing a steepening of the terrain, and can also be observed in the literature on Fig. 9, that shows the distortions on the movement pattern as a function of the terrain slope steepness and are compatible with an uphill gait pattern [3].

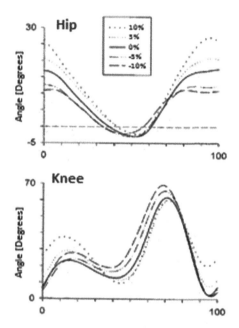

Fig. 9. Distortions on the movement pattern as a function of the terrain slope steepness.

Figure 10 shows the foot path, obtained from the generated gait shown in Fig. 7 applied to the leg's kinematic model with the hip joint as the reference point, supposing a 1.70 m height individual. The graph also shows the foot path for the same individual considering the biomechanical gait pattern obtained from the literature [2]. This graph 10 shows that the foot path generated by the artificial gait is consistent with the biomechanical gaits foot path, having similar shapes and amplitudes. The relatively smaller length step of the artificial gait could be easily corrected by adjusting the Swing signal amplitude.

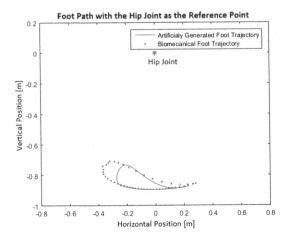

Fig. 10. Foot path, considering the hip joint as the reference point for the local coordinate system.

Another biomechanical gait cycle diagram with reference point on the hip joint is reproduced in Fig. 11 for comparison purposes with Lacquanit et al. [4].

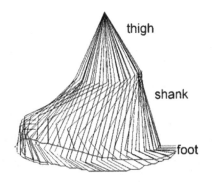

Fig. 11. Biomechanical gait cycle diagram.

Finally, when the same artificial gait pattern (Fig. 7) is applied to a two-legged kinematic model in the inertial reference system, feet paths consistent with steps can be observed (Fig. 12), revealing that a forward locomotion movement would be achieved with it.

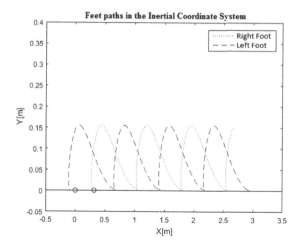

Fig. 12. Feet paths, in the inertial coordinate system.

6 Conclusion

This paper presented a cognitive approach to gait generation, inspired by algorithms such as Khatib's potential fields and elaborate architectures like AuRA.

One of the greatest advantages of the proposed architecture is its flexibility, which allows it to adapt the emergent gait cycle in real time for different terrains, according to the current perception input of the environment.

Another interesting feature of the proposal is that it is not limited to the humanoid legs and could be adapted to perform locomotion with other legs setups.

Even though the architecture is not yet fully implemented and need some improvement on parts like the hierarchic layer and data acquisition, the results of this study revealed that the superposition of signals can provide great results.

Although not identical, both artificial and biomechanical patterns show great similarities to each other. The kinematic simulation results showed that the artificial patterns are similar both in shape and amplitude to the biomechanical ones, and would probably perform a successful gait movement if applied to a dynamic model or a prototype. In addition to the simulation results, the experimental implementation confirmed visually some of the model results and revealed the embedding potential of the algorithm, which can be useful in future studies.

Because of its characteristics, this approach can also be expanded and further explored in future works.

It would be possible to expand the repertoire of basic behavior signals in a modular fashion. Since those signals run in parallel and are added together to form the output for the limbs, more behavior signals would allow for bigger combinations and for the generation of more complex movements, with functions that were not studied in this work (the balance maintenance problem, for instance).

Another possibility would be using machine learning methods, like neural networks for instance, to achieve optimal values for the parameters used by the artificial gait composition.

References

1. MacKay-Lyons, M.: Evidence of the central pattern generation of locomotion: a review. Phys. Ther. **82**(1), 69–83 (2002)
2. Leroux, A., Fung, J., Barbeau, H.: Adaptation of the walking pattern to uphill walking in normal and spinal-cord injured subjects. Exp. Brain Res. **126**, 359–368 (1999)
3. Leroux, A., Fung, J., Barbeau, H.: Postural adaptation to walking on inclined surfaces: I normal strategies. Gait Posture **15**, 64–74 (2002)
4. Lacquaniti, F., Grasso, R., Zago, M.: Motor patterns for walking. News Physiol. Sci. **14**, 168–174 (1999)
5. Khatib, O.: Real-time obstacle avoidance for manipulators and mobile robots. In: IEEE International Conference on Robotics and Automation, St. Louis, Missouri, 25–28 March 1990, pp. 500–505 (1985)
6. Viel, E.: Marcha Humana, a Corrida e o Salto. Manole, Paris (2000)
7. Vaughan, C., Davis, B., O'Connor, J.: Dynamics of Human Gait. Kiboho Publishers, Cape Town (1992)
8. Carvalho, J.: Amputações de membrosinferiores: embusca da plena reabilitação. Manole (2003)
9. Mafra, N.: Processamento de Sinal na Avaliação Clínica da Marcha Humana. Thesis (Master), 62 p., FEUP, Portugal, 26 Sept 2012
10. Rodacki, A.L.F.: Análise dos Fatores Antropométricos em Biomecânica. http://www.profedf.ufpr.br/rodackibiomecanica_arquivos/Parametros%20antropom%20em%20Biomecanica.pdf. Accessed 05 Feb 2014
11. Arkin, R.C., Balch, T.R.: AuRA: principles and practice in review. J. Exp. Theor. Artif. Intell. **9**(2) (1997)

Ocular Control Characterization of Motor Disabilities: The Cerebral Palsy Case

Jully González, Angélica Atehortúa, Ricardo Moncayo,
and Eduardo Romero$^{(\boxtimes)}$

CIM@LAB, Universidad Nacional de Colombia, Bogotá, Colombia
edromero@unal.edu.co

Abstract. Global statistics estimate 80% of people with disabilities live in developing countries, i.e., nearly 85 million people in Latin America and the Caribbean, being the most prevalent the motor disability, for instance 13 million cases in Brazil. Cerebral Palsy (CP) is considered as a public health problem and the most common cause of motor illness in children. Between 50–90% of the patients with this condition present visual problems, reason why this population exhibits visual sensory and motor abnormalities at rates exceeding those detected in neurologically normal children. This work proposes an automatic estimation of the ocular motion, an evaluation that might be extended to any kind of motor disorder. Visual patterns are quantified when challenging the ocular motor system by smooth and saccadic gaze tasks. The motion field obtained by a customized optical flow is characterized by velocity histograms of magnitude and orientation. The temporal result is accumulated in a histogram and a correlation distance between histograms quantifies the differences between subjects. Evaluation results showed significant differences between two PC and control groups constituted by 16 subjects each. This work introduces actual quantification of a prevalent disease whose evaluation and treatment so far if fully dependent on the examiner expertise.

Keywords: Cerebral palsy · Ocular motion · Optical flow · Characterization

1 Introduction

According to the World Health Organization, 10% of the population has some type of disability and 80% lives in developing countries. In Latin America and the Caribbean that figure would correspond to 85 million people [29]. In Colombia there about two and a half million people (6.3% of the population) with some permanent limitation [17]. Cerebral palsy (CP) describes a group of permanent disorders characterized by some kind of movement and posture abnormality, causing an activity limitation attributed to fetal or infant brain non progressive

Supported by Universidad Nacional de Colombia.

N. Lepore et al. (Eds.): SaMBa 2018, LNCS 11379, pp. 127–137, 2019.
https://doi.org/10.1007/978-3-030-13835-6_14

disturbances [25]. CP is considered the most common cause of physical disability in childhood [1,9,17,17]. CP is a highly cost disease, v.g., according to the Center of Disease Control and Prevention (CDC) a patient lifetime expenses may reach US 1.000.000 per CP patient [7].

This disease often presents dysfunction of the visual system [23]. Between 50–90% of patients with this condition shows visual problems, including refractive errors, strabismus, nystagmus, and amblyopia as well as cortical visual impairment [21], at rates far exceeding those detected in neurologically normal children [4,9,23]. CP diagnosis is currently based on both clinical observation and qualitative assessment of the degree of motor development [16].

Treatment for Cerebral Palsy based on qualitative assessments entails therapeutic challenges as formulating an individualized treatment plan according to the needs of each child [14].

Qualitative assessment generates variability among the experts to determine the best treatment for the patient, likewise the treatment is also evaluated subjectively, which may vary evaluation of the patient's evolution.

For this reason, there is a need to optimize treatment strategies for individual patients in order to lead to lifelong improvements in function and capabilities [19]. Quantification of clinical assessment could support treatment strategies for individual patients.

2   State of the Art

Few studies have tried to measure CP visual impairment because of the large intra and inter-examiner variability. There exists a limited number of works that quantify the ocular movement in CP.

Several studies have been devoted to characterize CP eye movements. Ghasia et al. [9] carried out an observational study by performing ophthalmic and neurologic examinations, finding that visual deficits differ between mild and severe CP. Barca et al. [2] evaluated oculomotor function in children with CP by ophtalmological and orthoptic assessments. These authors reported most children (97%) showed visual disturbances. Black et al. [3] clinically examined visual defects in various types of CP and informed children with this condition show higher incidence of ocular abnormalities. Dufresne et al. [5] introduced an statistical analysis based on parents' interview, clinical history, interpretation of neuroimaging data and visual observation of the patient stage. These studies agree about most CP patients present some degree of visual disturbances but none of them somehow quantify it.

On the other hand, some investigations have tried to quantify eye motion. Illavarason et al. [13] report improvement of Visual Evoked Potentials (VEP) in a group of 25 CP patients before and after therapy, yet their results were not compared with a control group. Ego et al. [6] recorded horizontal eye movements of the dominant eye using an infrared eye tracker (Eyelink 1000). Different smooth and saccadic visual tasks determined the performance of the CP patients and the control subjects. This work demonstrated CP ocular control improves with age. Nevertheless, this study failed at analyzing the binocular movement which is usually altered in CP. Kooiker *et al.* [15] proposed a method to quantify visual information by measuring visual orienting responses with an integrated infrared eye-tracking system (Tobii T60-XL). They evaluated the evolution in two different sessions and reported improvement in 80% of the CP children.

Other studies characterize the disease using eye tracking technologies. For example, Wong *et al.* [33] explore correlations between eye movement parameters with cognitive functions in Parkinson patients using an eye tracking device, obtaining ocular patterns in specific tests such as mean saccadic amplitude and mean fixation duration, both highly correlated with the cognitive decline in Parkinson's disease. Likewise, different studies perform ocular quantification using this type of technology. For example Schmidt *et al.* [26] and Hunt *et al.* [12] present a study of ocular motion in Parkinson's disease. Hong *et al.* [11] analyzed the eye gaze and pupillary response. A complete review of it can be found in Harezlak and Kasprowski [10]. However, these studies present a high susceptibility to the calibration process that is required to control the position of the eyes and calculate the direction of the gaze on a visual stimulus.

The main contribution of this work is an automatic characterization of the ocular motion that might be extended to any kind of motor disorder, performing an reliable quantification of a prevalent disease. This method gives a quantitative assessment that may contribute clinicians to perform a follow-up of the patient to provide a treatment according to the condition of each patient - personalized treatment.

3 Materials and Methods

3.1 Participants

Thirty two participants were involved in this research. Sixteen patients with CP and sixteen control children aged between 2 and 15 years. Participants were selected to constitute a study cohort depicted in the Table 1. This were compared by age and gender, with twenty males and twelve females, showing a homogeneous group. Some characteristics of the CP group can be seen in Table 2 including the GMFCS (Gross Motor Function Classification System)[20] level, which is used to characterize the functional severity of CP patients.

Table 1. Experimental population

	CP group		Control group	
Gender	M	F	M	F
Num. participants	10	6	10	6
Age[*years*]	6.9 ± 3.4	9.4 ± 3.2	6.7 ± 3.0	9.1 ± 3.2

Table 2. CP group general characteristics

GMFCS	# CP patients	Age[*years*]	Gender	
			Male	Female
Level 1	1	9	1	-
Level 2	1	7	-	1
Level 3	-	-	-	-
Level 4	4	9.7 ± 3.4	1	3
Level 5	10	6.9 ± 3.5	8	2

Selection process for CP cohort was performed taking into account following criteria: the patient must be able to sit in a chair, to maintain trunk and head with or without support, to follow instructions and to have cognitive skills.

CP participants belong to RIIE Rehabilitation Center in Bogotá, Colombia. Informed consents were obtained from the volunteers during the research, following the Helsinky convention [34], in which a complete description of the procedure was given to child's parents.

3.2   Acquisition

Two horizontal visual tasks were designed to attract patient's visual attention with the help of moving emoji as object in Fig. 1. A video capture of ocular motion is recorded with a medium speed camera (120 fps) hold in a helmet.

As studied population were children, a simple emoji was used to attract patient's attention by moving it over a black background (Fig. 1). Two tasks were evaluated: for the pursuing task, the emoji moved smoothly and horizontally over the background in a video of 30 s. While for the saccadic task, the emoji changed its position spontaneously in a video of 17 s.

Fig. 1. Smooth pursuing visual stimulus.

The horizontal ocular movement was chosen being this the easiest eye movement to control due to from the anatomical base the medial and lateral rectus muscles form an antagonistic pair that controls the horizontal position of each eye [24]. From which visual tasks were designed to evaluate the saccadic and smooth pursuit systems in the horizontal direction of the eye movement. These systems constitute most gaze-shifting mechanisms, where the smooth pursuit system allows the fovea to track a moving target as it slides across a stationary background and in the saccadic system gaze rapidly shifts from one point to another [24].

Performing the analysis of the ocular movement behavior of these two visual tasks, it is possible to find distinctive patterns for each experimental group (CP and Control).

3.3 Experimental Setup

A 32-inch screen, a child helmet and a speed camera were used for the experimentation. The helmet hold a GoPro Hero Session 5 camera which recorded the ocular motion at 120 fps. Anthropometric measures were taken into account to define the environment setup parameters during the video capture as illustrated in Fig. 2.

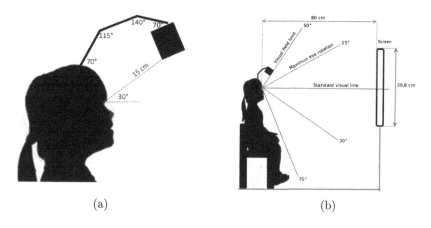

(a)   (b)

Fig. 2. Experimental setup.

The patient was located in front of the screen to perform the task. The sit was placed 80 cm far from the screen, aligning the eyes and mid-line of the screen, as shown in Fig. 2b. An extension arm, attached to the helmet, maintained the camera out of the visual field, as illustrated in Fig. 2a. In the experimental protocol, video capture and the visual tasks were synchronized for the ocular motion evaluation with all the participants.

3.4 Preprocessing

Viola Jones' Algorithm [31], is automatic detection system [32] widely used in facial and eye detection [30]. We used it to detect and get a ROI associated to the eyes. Then, a morphological reconstruction method [28] is applied on each ROI to automatically delimit the eye and thus obtain the ROI to be analyzed (Fig. 3). This is performed just in one frame in the video (where subject has both eyes opened) and then applied to the rest of the video; this given that as the camera is fixed the ROI does not change over the rest of the video.

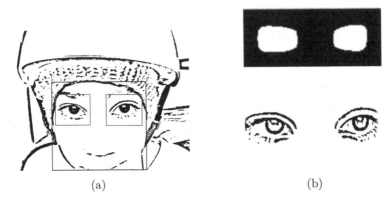

(a)   (b)

Fig. 3. Face and eye detection is performed by using Viola Jone's algorithm (a). Morphological reconstruction allows to refine the ROI (b).

3.5   Motion Description

From the detected region, the ocular motion is tracked using the optical flow approach. This method models the apparent motion as an independent per pixel motion between two consecutive frames at times t and $t + \Delta t$, as follows: $f(x, y, t) \approx f(x + \Delta x, y + \Delta y, t + \Delta t)$ where $f(x, y, t)$ is the intensity of the image at position (x, y) and at time t, and $(\Delta x, \Delta y)$ is the pixel displacement in the time interval Δt. Optical flow equation is then obtained:

$$\nabla I \bullet P + I_t = 0$$

where $\nabla I = (I_x, I_y)$ is the spatial gradient, $P = (\Delta x, \Delta y)$ is the displacement field and I_t is the temporal derivative. [18] This equation relates the velocity to the space-time image derivatives at one image location [8]. The Lucas-Kanade method [22] solves the basic optical flow equations by a least squares criterion. This algorithm provides an estimate of the movement of interesting features in successive images of a scene.

3.6   Motion Histogram

Magnitude and orientation histograms are computed from the obtained velocity vectors along the time for each visual task. Histograms display the relative frequency of velocity data values and its temporal distribution. Velocity vectors between 75° to 105° and 255° to 285° were discarded from the analysis since they correspond to the eyelid movements.

4   Results

Velocity histograms characterized the ocular movement during the smooth pursuit and saccadic visual tasks in all participants. Estimation of relative ocular motion among the participants was performed by measuring the distance between velocity histograms using the cosine distance [27] as a measure of similarity. This measure indicates how close two histograms in the same direction are by performing a dot product between the two histograms. Velocity magnitudes are hereafter shown for the two pursuit task:

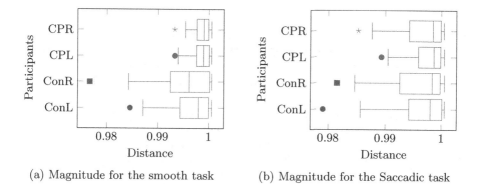

(a) Magnitude for the smooth task   (b) Magnitude for the Saccadic task

Fig. 4. Box plots of the velocity magnitude for the CP group (blue boxes) and Control group (red boxes). Panels (a) and (b) show the box plots for smooth pursuit and saccadic tasks. (Color figure online)

Figure 4 shows the obtained histogram distances corresponding to the velocity magnitude during both tracking tasks: smooth and saccadic for the PC and control groups (R and L conventions stand for right and left eye). Basically, this plot is showing how variable the velocity is during the particular task. It is observable the largest variability of the PC group for the smooth task, probably meaning that this pursuit task requires a more exigent control which starts to be lost by the PC group. In contrast, these differences are less clear for the saccadic task, likely because the level of control required in such situation is much less important.

Likewise, the distance between orientation histograms is plotted in Fig. 5 for both visual tasks. In each figure, the experimental groups are referred by their abbreviation: CPR - Right eye in Cerebral Palsy group, CPL - Left eye in Cerebral Palsy group, ConR - Right eye in control group and ConL - Left eye in control group.

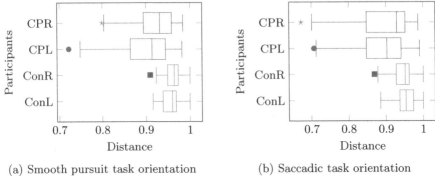

(a) Smooth pursuit task orientation   (b) Saccadic task orientation

Fig. 5. Box plots corresponding to orientation results during both visual tasks for the whole experimental group. Panels (a) and (b) display the box plot for smooth pursuit task and saccadic task.

On the other hand, Fig. 5a the box plots of the distances between histograms of orientations. A first remarkable observation is that the PC group shows a largest data scattering, an observation attributed to the lose of visual control in this patient. In contrast with the magnitude estimation, this difference is also observed for the saccadic task.

Wilcoxon test was applied to compare the two experimental groups: CP and control. Magnitude comparison (right and left eyes) using this test shows statistically significant differences ($p < 0.05$). These statistical differences were not obtained for the saccadic task (both eyes). Likewise, orientation distances were also evaluated and they showed to be significant ($p < 0.01$).

4.1 Discussion

This work has introduced an automatic ocular motion characterization of the Cerebral Palsy. Our results demonstrate it was possible to identify quantifiable differences between CP and control groups during eye tracking of two visual tasks.

These results also showed significant differences between the CP and Control groups. They were however more evident in the smooth pursuit visual task. In contrast, the saccadic task limited the expression of the control system since the fixation mechanism was challenged during few moments of the visual task, basically a couple of acceleration and decelerations to track the target. The orientation evaluation showed larger differences between the two groups. It is very likely this type of tasks is more challenging for the control system and eventually a quantitative scale that objectively can follow-up the treatment for each patient with CP.

5   Conclusions

This work presents an automatic ocular motion characterization of Cerebral Palsy. The proposed method employs the optical flow and challenges the ocular control system with gaze pursuing tasks. The results show oculomotor control limitations in CP children. This quantitative and objective measurement may support clinicians to perform a follow-up of the patient and provide a personalized treatment.

References

1. Alimovic, S.: Visual impairments in childen with cerebral palsy. Hrvatska revija za rehabilitacijska istrazivanja **48**, 96–103 (2012). https://hrcak.srce.hr/file/117416
2. Barca, L., Cappelli, F.R., Di Giulio, P., Staccioli, S., Castelli, E.: Outpatient assessment of neurovisual functions in children with cerebral palsy. Res. Dev. Disabil. **31**(2), 488–495 (2010). https://doi.org/10.1016/j.ridd.2009.10.019
3. Black, P.D.: Ocular defects in children with cerebral palsy. Br. Med. J. **281**(6238), 487–488 (1980). https://doi.org/10.4103/0301-4738.33837
4. Breakey, A.S.: Ocular findings in cerebral palsy. Arch. Ophthalmol. **53**(6), 852–856 (1955). https://doi.org/10.1001/archopht.1955.00930010860011
5. Dufresne, D., Dagenais, L., Shevell, M.I.: Spectrum of visual disorders in a population-based cerebral palsy cohort. Pediatr. Neurol. **50**(4), 324–328 (2014). https://doi.org/10.1016/j.pediatrneurol.2013.11.022
6. Ego, C., Orban de Xivry, J.J., Nassogne, M.C., Yüksel, D., Lefèvre, P.: Spontaneous improvement in oculomotor function of children with cerebral palsy. Res. Dev. Disabil. **36**, 630–644 (2015). https://doi.org/10.1016/j.ridd.2014.10.025
7. Ferluga, E.D., et al.: Interventions for feeding and nutrition in cerebral palsy, No. 94, 43 (2013). Report No. 13-EHC015-EF. www.effectivehealthcare.ahrq.gov/reports/final.cfm
8. Fleet, D., Weiss, Y.: Optical flow estimation. In: Mathematical Models for Computer Vision: The Handbook, pp. 239–257 (2005). https://doi.org/10.1109/TIP.2009.2032341, http://eprints.pascal-network.org/archive/00001065/
9. Ghasia, F., Brunstrom, J., Gordon, M., Tychsen, L.: Frequency and severity of visual sensory and motor deficits in children with cerebral palsy: gross motor function classification scale. Invest. Ophthalmol. Vis. Sci. **49**(2), 572–580 (2008). https://doi.org/10.1167/iovs.07-0525
10. Harezlak, K., Kasprowski, P.: Application of eye tracking in medicine: a survey, research issues and challenges. Comput. Med. Imaging Graph. **65**, 176–190 (2018). https://doi.org/10.1016/j.compmedimag.2017.04.006
11. Hong, M.P., et al.: Eye gaze and pupillary response in Angelman syndrome. Res. Dev. Disabil. **68**(July), 88–94 (2017). https://doi.org/10.1016/j.ridd.2017.06.011
12. Hunt, D., et al.: Do people with Parkinson's disease look at task relevant stimuli when walking? An exploration of eye movements. Behav. Brain Res. **348**, 82–89 (2018). https://doi.org/10.1016/j.bbr.2018.03.003
13. Illavarason, P., Arokia Renjit, J., Mohan Kumar, P.: Clinical evaluation of functional vision assessment by utilizing the visual evoked potential device for cerebral palsy rehabilitation. Procedia Comput. Sci. **132**, 128–140 (2018). https://doi.org/10.1016/j.procs.2018.05.174

14. Jan, M.: Cerebral palsy: comprehensive review and update. Ann. Saudi Med. **26**(2), 123–132 (2006). https://doi.org/10.5144/0256-4947.2006.123

15. Kooiker, M.J.G., van der Steen, J., Pel, J.J.M.: Reliability of visual orienting response measures in children with and without visual impairments. J. Neurosci. Methods **233**, 54–62 (2014). https://doi.org/10.1016/j.jneumeth.2014.06.005

16. Krigger, K.W.: Cerebral palsy: an overview. Am. Fam. Physician **73**(1), 91–100 (2006). http://www.ncbi.nlm.nih.gov/pubmed/16417071

17. Martínez Marín, R.d.P., Angarita Fonseca, A., Rojas Gutiérrez, M., Rojas Pérez, K., Velandia Rojas, E.: Caracterización de la discapacidad de una muestra de niños con Parálisis Cerebral de Bucaramanga y su area metropolitana, Colombia (2013). https://revistas.unal.edu.co/index.php/revfacmed/article/view/39694/47271

18. O'Donovan, P.: Optical flow: techniques and applications. Int. J. Comput. Vis. pp. 1–26 (2005). http://www.dgp.toronto.edu/~donovan/stabilization/opticalflow.pdf

19. Pagnozzi, A.M., et al.: The need for improved brain lesion segmentation techniques for children with cerebral palsy: a review. Int. J. Dev. Neurosci. **47**, 229–246 (2015). https://doi.org/10.1016/j.ijdevneu.2015.08.004

20. Palisano, R., Rosenbaum, P., Bartlett, D., Livingstone, M., Walter, S., Russell, D.: Gross motor function classification system. McMaster Univ. (Dev. Med. Chile. Neurol.) **39**, 214–233 (1997)

21. Park, M.J., Yoo, Y.J., Chung, C.Y., Hwang, J.M.: Ocular findings in patients with spastic type cerebral palsy. BMC Ophthalmol. **16**(1), 195 (2016). https://doi.org/10.1186/s12886-016-0367-1

22. Patel, D., Saurahb, U.: Optical flow measurement using Lucas Kanade method. Int. J. Comput. Appl. **61**(10), 6–10 (2013)

23. Porro, G., van der Linden, D., van Nieuwenhuizen, O., Wittebol-Post, D.: Role of visual dysfunction in postural control in children with cerebral palsy. Neural plast. **12**(2–3), 205–210 (2005). https://www.ncbi.nlm.nih.gov/pmc/articles/PMC2565462/

24. Krauzlis, R.J.: Fundamental neuroscience. In: Fundamental Neuroscience: chap. 32 Eye Mov, 4th edn, pp. 697–714 (2013). https://doi.org/10.1016/B978-0-12-385870-2.00032-9

25. Rosenbaum, P., et al.: A report: the definition and classification of cerebral palsy April 2006. Dev. Med. Child Neurol. **49**(109), 8–14 (2007). https://doi.org/10.1111/j.1469-8749.2007.tb12610.x

26. Schmidt, K., Gamer, M., Forkmann, K., Bingel, U.: Pain affects visual orientation: an eye-tracking study. J. Pain **19**(2), 135–145 (2018). https://doi.org/10.1016/j.jpain.2017.09.005

27. Sinha, A.K., Shukla, K.K.: A study of distance metrics in histogram based image retrieval academic discipline and sub-disciplines. Int. J. Comput. Technol. **4**(3), 821–830 (2013). https://doi.org/10.24297/ijct.v4i3.4205

28. Soille, P.: Morphological Image Analysis: Principles and Applications. Springer, Heidelberg (1999). https://doi.org/10.1007/978-3-662-03939-7

29. Vásquez, A.: La discapacidad en América Latina. Discapacidad. Lo que todos debemos saber 9–23 (2006). http://www.paho.org/Spanish/DD/PUB/Discapacidad-SPA.pdf

30. Vikram, K.: Facial parts detection using viola. In: 2017 4th International Conference on Advanced Computing and Communication Systems (ICACCS), pp. 2015–2018 (2017). https://doi.org/10.1109/ICACCS.2017.8014636

31. Viola, P., Jones, M.J.: Robust real-time face detection. Int. J. Comput. Vis. **57**(2), 137–154 (2004). https://doi.org/10.1023/B:VISI.0000013087.49260.fb

32. Wang, Y.Q.: An analysis of the viola-jones face detection algorithm. Image Process. On Line **4**, 128–148 (2014). https://doi.org/10.5201/ipol.2014.104
33. Wong, O.W., et al.: Eye movement parameters and cognitive functions in Parkinson's disease patients without dementia. Parkinsonism Relat. Disord. **52**, 43–48 (2018). https://doi.org/10.1016/j.parkreldis.2018.03.013
34. World Medical Association: World Medical Association Declaration of Helsinki. Ethical principles for medical research involving human subjects. Bull. World Health Organ. **79**(4), 373–374 (2001). https://doi.org/S0042--96862001000400016 [pii]

Author Index

Printed in the United States
By Bookmasters